To Syd

The BH War Poet
and author of the
poem, 'Alone I Remember'

With Best Wishes,

Peter Twist
London November 2020.

Overtones of War

EDMUND BLUNDEN

Overtones of War

Poems of the First World War

Edited with an Introduction
by
Martin Taylor

Duckworth

First published in 1996 by
Gerald Duckworth & Co. Ltd.
The Old Piano Factory
48 Hoxton Square, London N1 6PB
Tel: 0171 729 5986
Fax: 0171 729 0015

A catalogue record for this book is available
from the British Library.

ISBN 0 7156 2739 2

Typeset by Ray Davies
Printed in Great Britain by
Redwood Books Ltd, Trowbridge

Dedicated to
Amanda Stembridge
(1957-1993)

CONTENTS

ACKNOWLEDGEMENTS

My principal thanks must be to Claire Blunden, who has supported this project from its conception. I am grateful also to Barry Webb and Dominic Hibberd for their advice, to Robin Baird-Smith for his patience, and to David Goudge, without whose help and affection this book would not have been possible.

INTRODUCTION

The idea for this collection came in March 1993 during an event at the Imperial War Museum to mark the centenary of the birth of Wilfred Owen. On that occasion the address was given by the late Sir Stephen Spender, who paid tribute to the poets of the First World War and to their ability to transform the extremes of experience into art. Included in his speech was a roll call of the significant names, beginning with Wilfred Owen, and embracing Siegfried Sassoon, David Jones, Herbert Read, Ivor Gurney, and Isaac Rosenberg. But there was one important omission from this list: Sir Stephen had left out the name of Edmund Blunden.

Inadvertent or otherwise, this seemed all too symbolic of a wider disregard of Edmund Blunden's work. Almost all of the major First World War poets have some sort of appreciation society, and although there have been several excellent critical studies and recently an authoritative biography, other than the verse appendix to *Undertones of War* only a small selection of his poems is currently available.

This collection then needs no excuse. Indeed it is surprising that there has been no previous edition of war poems, given that Blunden was one the most dedicated of First World War commentators. No other participant had written so extensively and so movingly about the conflict, its 'Impacts and Delayed Actions'; no one had been more concerned with its aftertones as well as its undertones. He was one of the last surviving major war writers, many of whom he served faithfully as editor and critic; but it was at the call of his own war memories that he served longest and most diligently. Published on the centenary of his birth, this collection is a tribute to that service.

It is not intended to be a definitive collection: it includes, with one exception, only published work. No attempt has been made to consult the various Blunden archives – the largest being the 110 boxes held by the Harry Ransom Humanities Research Center at the University of Texas. Neither are included all poems containing reference to the First World War. A.E. Housman wrote to Gilbert Murray in 1922: 'I have been admiring Blunden for some time. He describes too much; but when one describes so well, the temptation must be great';[1] and although nothing Blunden wrote about the war can be without interest, the temptation to be all-inclusive, inevitably to his detriment, is to be resisted.

[1] Quoted in Richard Perceval Graves, *A.E. Housman: The Scholar Poet*, Oxford, OUP, 1981, p. 232.

1

The term 'war poem' is in itself an ambiguous one. Does it only mean poems written in wartime, or any poem with war as its theme? Does it include therefore all poems written in wartime whatever their subject, and post-war poems which are not about the conflict but which betray its influence? In the end I have followed my own inclinations: only those pre-war service poems which mention the war are included, but all poems written during war service are collected. Also included are those post-war poems either directly about the war or overwhelmingly informed by it. This last distinction has been the most difficult to exercise. The effect of the First World War on Blunden was profound, affecting not only his moral outlook but also his creative voice. Thus many of his poems are, in Robyn Marsack's words, 'honey-combed with martial vocabulary and meaning', and others, while containing no specific reference to the conflict, are clearly subject to its enduring legacy.[2] For this reason I have chosen as a title *Overtones of War*, partly in homage to Blunden's First World War memoir, but also because the implication or suggestion of war is present throughout much of his work.

As far as possible I have arranged the poems in order of composition, but as there are great difficulties with the precise dating of Blunden's poems I have used date of first publication where a date of composition is not available from the text as published or other sources. I have also attempted, wherever possible, to respect the sequence given by Blunden in his original and collected editions of verse. For the dates of publication I owe an immense debt to B.J. Kirkpatrick's *A Bibliography of Edmund Blunden*; as I do to the late W.C. Chau, whose typescript *The Collected Poems of Edmund Blunden* has saved much time and energy, especially with those poems published only in periodicals and newspapers.[3]

Unless otherwise stated, the notes following some of the poems are the poet's, principally taken from his copies of *Undertones of War* (annotated for Aki Hayashi in April 1929) and *Poems 1914-30* (annotated in 1954 for a projected selected edition of 1955); the poet's variants of language and punctuation from the latter volume have been followed, and where they occur the relevant poems are marked by an asterisk.[4] Details of the place and date of first publication in periodical and book for each poem follow the notes. These and all other editorial annotations appear in square brackets, while Blunden's own handwritten notes, often added years after the writing of a poem, appear immediately below the poem concerned.

[2] *Edmund Blunden: selected poems*, edited by Robyn Marsack, Manchester, Carcanet, 1982, p. 5.

[3] B.J. Kirkpatrick, *A Bibliography of Edmund Blunden*, Oxford, Clarendon Press, 1979; *The Collected Poems of Edmund Blunden*, edited by W.C. Chau, typescript, n.d.

[4] Edmund Blunden, *Undertones of War*, London, Cobden-Sanderson, 1928; Edmund Blunden, *The Poems of Edmund Blunden* [spine reads: *Poems 1914-30*], London, Cobden-Sanderson, 1930.

Edmund Charles Blunden was born at 54a Tottenham Court Road, London on 1 November 1896. His urban residency, however, was short-lived: in 1900 his father, a teacher, was appointed headmaster of a Church of England primary school in Yalding, Kent, a place that was to become the nexus of Blunden's poetic imagination. An idyllic childhood in Yalding and the surrounding villages was interrupted in September 1909 when he took up a scholarship at Christ's Hospital, Horsham, Sussex. These two early influences of countryside and school were to dominate Blunden's poetry; as Barry Webb observes: 'As Yalding represented an ideal of rural simplicity, so Christ's Hospital became a symbol of sophisticated culture. These two contrasting elements were often in tension within Edmund, finding a partial resolution in the composition of poetry evoking simple pastoral scenes in rhetorical literary vocabulary and form.'[5]

It was at Christ's Hospital that Blunden became a confirmed poet, publishing first in the school magazine, *The Blue*, and then two privately printed pamphlets, *Poems Translated from the French* and *Poems*.[6] Of these early poems only one, 'October 1914', acknowledged that war that had broken out in August 1914; but although the conflict was not as yet a subject fit for verse, it was an inescapable fact of life, and in August 1915, having completed his secondary education and secured a place at Queen's College, Oxford, Blunden applied for and received a commission in the Royal Sussex Regiment.

During training in 1916 Blunden published four volumes of poetry in celebration of the rural scene – *The Barn*, *Three Poems*, *The Harbingers* (the previous two volumes combined) and *Pastorals* – as if he was trying to fix his feelings for the English countryside before he was sent overseas.[7] As the title of the last volume indicates, the poems were all in the pastoral tradition of English verse. Indeed Blunden was one the last exponents of that tradition, for he began to write just in time to witness the final disappearance of the old rustic order; even from strongholds in Kent where the ancient way of life could still seem eternal.

The rural order Blunden mourned was based on no fanciful ideal, but on existence as he knew it from his early years in Yalding, where he found 'a relationship of various talents and masteries, and courteous differences, which composed a serene, just kind of life.'[8] It was a life that was not only 'a picturesque spectacle, but a social idea.'[9] As an idea it may have been

[5] Barry Webb, *Edmund Blunden: a biography*, London, Yale University Press, 1990, p. 28.
[6] E.C. Blunden, *Poems*, Horsham, Price & Co. (printer), 1914; E.C. Blunden, *Poems translated from the French*, Horsham, Price & Co. (printer), 1914.
[7] E.C. Blunden, *The Barn*, Uckfield, J. Brooker (printer), 1916; E.C. Blunden, *[Three Poems]*, Uckfield, J. Brooker (printer), 1916; E.C. Blunden, *The Harbingers*, Uckfield, G.A. Blunden, 1916; E.C. Blunden, *Pastorals*, London, Erskine Macdonald, 1916.
[8] Edmund Blunden, 'The English Countryside', *The Mind's Eye: Essays*, London, Jonathan Cape, 1934, p. 157.
[9] Edmund Blunden, *The Face of England*, London, Longmans, Green, 1932, p. 109.

conservative, even feudal, but its reality gave Blunden the means to evaluate and survive his later experiences. In fact the old rural order was something that Blunden found satisfyingly present in army life. Reminiscing about the past in *Fall In, Ghosts*, an account of a battalion reunion published in June 1932, he recalled: 'I have seen many varieties of beautiful simplicity in my life ... With such treasures I count the voluntary, sweet and accomplished courtesy which I see in a reunion from men to the officers – and from them again, in another and equally valuable sense, to the men.'[10]

The less attractive aspects of the old rural order also seemed to anticipate Blunden's future in his early poem 'The Barn' (not reprinted here). Although written in 1916 before his departure for France, the poem reads like an allegory of his military career. A Job-like farmer is visited by a series of catastrophes – failed crops, storm damage – but remains resilient in the face of disaster. His fortitude is rewarded with the restoration of his fortunes, only to find that his experiences have alienated him from his former acquaintances. Or as Blunden later wrote in his *War Poets* pamphlet: 'The old Great War ended, and one trouble that followed was that Peace was not all happiness'.[11]

'The Barn' is also a symbol of the irrevocable change in rural life, a celebration of its existence, and an acknowledgement of its dissolution. For like Hardy, Blunden was an elegist for a world that was passing away; undermined by urbanization and industrialization, and the repercussions of the First World War. No other poet of the period eulogised rural life as powerfully as Blunden in his early poetry and in the post-war volumes *The Waggoner* (1920), *The Shepherd* (1922), *To Nature* (1923), and *English Poems* (1925), partly written before the conflict but largely later, in passionate recollection of what had been lost.[12] (His annotated copy of *Poems 1914-1930* contains many notes indicating the places and often the pre-war dates of the scenes that inspired the poems in these volumes.) But the effect of passionate recollection could be dangerous: Blunden's observation of Ivor Gurney that 'The immense love of his country which [his] experiences as a child and as a youth implanted what was to become almost as a tyranny over his poetical character' was as true of Blunden as it was of Gurney.

Discussing *The Shepherd* in the chapter of *New Bearings in English Poetry* (1932) entitled 'The Situation at the End of the First World War', F.R. Leavis acknowledged that this quality of passionate recollection set

[10] Edmund Blunden, 'Fall In, Ghosts', *Edmund Blunden: a selection of his poetry and prose*, edited by Kenneth Hopkins, London, Rupert Hart-Davis, 1950, pp. 250-251.

[11] Edmund Blunden, *War Poets 1914-1918*, London, Longmans, Green, 1958, p. 31.

[12] Edmund Blunden, *The Waggoner: and other poems*, Sidgwick & Jackson, 1920; Edmund Blunden, *The Shepherd: and other poems of peace and war*, London, Cobden-Sanderson, 1922; Edmund Blunden, *To Nature*, London, Cyril William Beaumont (printer), 1923; Edmund Blunden, *English Poems*, London, Cobden-Sanderson, 1926.

Blunden apart from the rural poets of his generation: 'out of the traditional life of the English countryside, especially as relived in memories of childhood, Mr Blunden was creating a world – a world in which to find refuge from adult distresses; above all, one guessed, from memories of war ... He was able to be, to some purpose, conservative in his technique, and draw upon the eighteenth century, because the immemorial rural order was real to him.'[13] Although there are war poems in both *The Waggoner* and *The Shepherd*, the titles of these collections as much as their contents indicate that Blunden identified himself as a rural poet (a label he later came to resent), and it is significant that upon his release from the army, Blunden sent Sassoon – the then acknowledged 'war poet' and the newly appointed editor of the *Daily Herald* – not his war verse but his early 1916 volumes of pastoral verse.

The pastoral has a long history, dating back to Theocritus in the third century B.C., but it was Vergil's *Ecologues* which gave the form its importance. In common with most subsequent pastoral poets, Vergil lived in an urban society and his poems spring from the townsman's dream of a golden age in which men minded their flocks in peace and simplicity. The word 'pastoral' literally means 'concerning shepherds'; hence Blunden's self-appellation, 'a harmless young shepherd in a soldier's coat', which fuses the conflicting demands of pastoralism and war.[14] The pastoral tradition inherited by Blunden owed most to its eighteenth-century manifestation, as practised by poets like George Crabbe, Thomas Gray, John Clare, Edward Young, and Wordsworth. It usually contrasted simple and complicated life, to the advantage of the former, in a rural setting, close to the elemental rhythms of nature – an ordered image of civilization, of man in harmony with his environment. Of the pastoral poets of the eighteenth century it was with John Clare that Blunden claimed greatest kinship. (In France, as he records in *Undertones of War*, he spent many hours reading and re-reading Young and Clare. Young's voice, 'speaking out of a profound eighteenth-century calm', helped to maintain his sanity; Clare's life, as celebrated in 'Clare's Ghost' – written by Blunden in the trenches – helped to put his current existence into perspective.)[15] According to John H. Johnston: 'Blunden's description of natural scenes, like Clare's, is fresh and spontaneous; his lyrical gift accommodates itself to the external reality rather than to romantic flights of imagination suggested by reality. Blunden's diction, too, resembles Clare's; simple and unpretentious, it is often invigorated by the use of dialectical words that reflect the poet's effort to assimilate the language as well as the landscape of his native region.'[16]

It is this rootedness in the English scene, both actual (as a true resident

[13] F.R. Leavis, *New Bearings in English Poetry*, London, Chatto & Windus, 1932, pp. 66-67.
[14] *Undertones*, p. 266.
[15] Ibid., p. 236.
[16] John H. Johnston, *Poetry of the First World War: a study of the evolution of lyric and narrative form*, Princeton: Princeton University Press, 1964, p. 117.

of the countryside) and literary (as a dedicated student of pastoral poetry), that enabled Blunden to escape 'the weekend-cottage view of nature of the typical Georgian.'[17] What distinguishes Blunden from Georgian poets like Ralph Hodgson, James Stephens, and Andrew Young (published, like Blunden, in Edward Marsh's *Georgian Poetry* series) is the intensity of his absorption in rural life; a quality matched in his contemporaries only by Edward Thomas and Ivor Gurney. It was in writing about Ivor Gurney that Blunden put his finger on the weaknesses of Georgian poetry: 'neither easy sentiment nor an indifferent "eye on the object" can be imputed to him, nor yet languor nor studied homeliness of expression.'[18] This is equally true of Blunden's best work, and particularly so of his war poems.

From his arrival in France in May 1916 Blunden wrote poetry regularly (collected here under the heading 'The Shepherd at War'). He remembered later:

Among the multitudes of us shipped to the Pas de Calais a few months before the Great Push (or Drive) of the British Army in 1916, I was a verse-writer; my interests were not yet changed from what life had formed before all this chaos. Lurking in the trenches by day or prowling out of them at night, I would perforce know what a bedevilled world is, and yet to make poems about it was a puzzle. In May and June 1916, in my notebooks, the grimness of war began to compete as a subject with the pastorals of peace. By the end of the year, when madness seemed totally to rule the hour, I was almost a poet of the shell-holes, of ruin and mortification. But the stanzas then written were left in the pocket-book: what good were they, who cared, who would agree?[19]

Blunden published only three poems during his time in France: 'The Dancer in Thrall', 'The Cook's Story', and 'Phantasies' (later re-titled 'Clare's Ghost'). These appeared in *The Blue*, but, perhaps out of consideration for his old school's sensibilities or because of his own diffidence, they were not the poems of 'shell-holes, of ruin and mortification' which remained unpublished until after the war. Blunden came across very little contemporary poetry sympathetic to his changing outlook during the war years. He did read Sassoon with excitement in the *Cambridge Magazine* of July 1917, and Robert Nichols, but realised that Sassoon's savage ironies and Nichols' lyric outpourings were not paths he could follow. More typical of the poets he came across was Robert Service, characterised by Blunden as 'one of Britain's he-poets', and Gilbert Frankau, in whose style

[17] Bernard Bergonzi, *Heroes' Twilight: a study of the literature of the Great War*, London, Constable, 1965, p. 68.
[18] *Poems by Ivor Gurney: principally selected from unpublished manuscripts*, with a memoir by Edmund Blunden, London, Hutchinson, 1954, p. 19.
[19] Blunden, *War Poets*, pp. 26-27.

Blunden wrote 'The Cook's Story'. Knowledge of Wilfred Owen, Edward Thomas, Ivor Gurney, and Isaac Rosenberg was only to come after the Armistice.[20]

Blunden's early poems of 1916 do alternate between celebrations of the rural scene and realistic descriptions of France, with the latter becoming the dominant subject towards the end of the year and thereafter. 'The Dancer in Thrall', published in *The Blue* in December 1916, is an allegory of this poetic sea change. Although not a good poem – Blunden never reprinted it – it is a revealing one, which recognises that the war has made the retreat into pastoralism no longer an adequate response.

> Who then with curbing hands like chains
> Of carking iron shackled me,
> And jarred my songs to motes and grains,
> And lamed my light-heeled revelry?

Blunden's war poems of this period are not based on any revolution in style, technique or attitude, as with Sassoon and Owen, but rather on an adaptation of pastoralism to his new experiences. The understated style he had developed for his pastoral poetry took on a more ironic tone and perspective, but he was not seduced into an explicitness or a savagery he could not have sustained. Neither would it have been appropriate, for Blunden's talents lay elsewhere. His ability to describe scenes of war through the eyes of a pastoral poet is the source of his emotional stability and his imaginative freedom. By adapting his poetry to his circumstances he was not overwhelmed by them. Instead he attains a balance both in language – when he describes the beauties of nature his phrasing is that of a pastoral poet; when he describes the effects of war his vocabulary reflects the violence of the scene – and sensibility – the power of pastoralism is diminished because the reality of war is overwhelming.

> And all the old delight is cursed
> Redoubling present undelight.
> Splinter, crystal, splinter and burst;
> And sear no more with second sight.
> 'In Festubert'

Nature can provide a temporary refuge from war but not an escape; although it still represents a moral force, an ideal. That its harmony has been disrupted is in itself an indictment of war. Through the poet, the war is seen and judged by Nature. In the poem of the same title, the trees on the Calais Road voice that judgement:

[20] Blunden, *Undertones of War*, p. 8.

> With natural dole and lamentation
> They groan for the slaughter and desecration,
> But every moment adds to the cry
> Of that dead army driving by.

The surviving poems of 1917 – Blunden records that those he wrote in the summer of that year 'vanished in the mud' – share a characteristic pattern: the setting is usually out of action, but with the memory or promise of action very near.[21] Although there is no attempt to deal with action, its very proximity gives the snatched moments of comparative peace a terrible poignancy.

> Now to attune my dull soul, if I can,
> To the contentment of this countryside
> Where man is not for ever killing man
> But quiet days like these calm waters glide.
> 'Bleue Maison'

Nature is still looked to by the poet as a source of inspiration or comfort, but the reality of war is too close to sustain complete faith. Even 'The Unchangeable', which asserts the benevolent power of Nature, compromises its optimism by the unanswered question with which it concludes.

> Why do you leave my woods untrod so long?
> Still float the bronze carp on my lilied lakes,
> Still the wood-fairies round my spring wells throng;
> And chancing lights on willowy waterbreaks
> Dance to the bubbling brooks of elfin song.

Although Blunden later wrote in the *War Poets* pamphlet: 'if you were a soldier-poet not blown to bits, you might not find the words for the protest against those sorrows; you might still be moved instinctively to recall the healing presences of the world you had known', his poems of the war years show that the act of recall did not always bring the comfort it promised.[22] Zillebeke Brook, in the poem of that title, reminds Blunden of 'a glassy burn / Ribanded through a brake of Kentish fern', but the memory only serves to emphasise the pain of his present situation:

> And much too clear you bring it back to me,
> You dreary brook deformed with cruelty,
> Here where I halt to catch the day's best mood,
> On my way up to Sanctuary Wood.
> 'Zillebeke Brook'

[21] Blunden, 'Preface', *Poems 1914-30*, p. v.
[22] Op. cit., p. 26.

Although not poems of rebellion, these poems of the war years do express
protest in that they detail the effects of the conflict on the countryside of
France. Even a poem like 'The Sighing Time', ostensibly about the reput-
edly haunted Blunden family home at Congelow, takes on a critical hue if
read allegorically. Like Owen's 'The Kind Ghosts', 'The Sighing Time' is
about the cost of the war to an uncomprehending England, represented in
'The Kind Ghosts' by the sleeping Britannia figure and in 'The Sighing
Time' by 'the old house'.

Blunden's active service effectively came to an end in February 1918
when he was posted to six months' duty in England, although he did return
to France after the Armistice for service with the occupation forces until
his demobilization in February 1919. During his service in France he
spent more time at the front than any other recognised war writer. Only
David Jones' 22 months can approach Blunden's two years. It is ironic,
therefore, that his writing should deal less with life in the front-line than
those of his contemporaries. His two years included some of the most
violent fighting in the war: at the Ancre and around Thiepval Wood in
August 1916 (he won a Military Cross for operations at the Schwaben
Redoubt on 13 November 1916 – a fact he neglects to mention in *Undertones of War*), and the Battle of Third Ypres (or Passchendaele) launched
on 3 June 1917. *Undertones of War* is essential reading for details of
Blunden's military service, and a clear account of his battalion's activities
is also given in 'A Battalion History', reprinted here from his 1934 volume
of essays *The Mind's Eye*.

The poems in 'The Shepherd Returns' section show how much the war
affected Blunden's response to nature. In 'A Country God' (written by
Blunden in February 1918 on leaving France) the poet contrasts his
former self, a pastoral poet close to the rhythms of nature, with his current
self, a ghost alienated from his home and the past by his experiences:

> But now the sower's hand is writhed
>   In livid death, the bright rhythm stolen,
> The gold grain flatted and unscythed,
>   The boars in the vineyard gnarled and sullen
> Havocking the grapes; and the pouncing wind
>   Spins the spattered leaves of the glen
> In a mockery dance, death's hue-and-cry;
> With all my murmurous pipes flung by
>   And summer not to come again.

Upon his return Blunden attended a training camp at Stowlangtoft, by
Stowmarket, Suffolk, where he wrote, in direct contrast to 'A Country
God', 'Wild Cherry Tree' and 'A Vignette'. 'Wild Cherry Tree' is an ecstatic
paean to the rural setting of the camp, almost too ecstatic, as if the war
had never happened, or perhaps in nervous reaction to his removal from

the front. This mood was not to last, and the period up to his demobilization – despite his marriage in June to Mary Daines, a young country girl
– was not a happy time. It was also his worst year for poetry: 'I'd been
keeping it up in the trenches and so on, then suddenly 1918 seemed to me
the blackest of the lot. (And yet we won the war!) I found the whole military
business suddenly too dull for poetry.'[23] Clearly Blunden was suffering
from some sort of delayed shell-shock or post-military depression; he later
remembered:

> Looking back over 1918 and this opening quarter of 1919, I became
> desperately confused over war and peace. Clearly, no man who knew
> and felt could wish for a second that the war should have lasted for
> a second longer. But, where it was not, and where the traditions and
> government which it had called into being had ceased to be, we who
> had been brought up to it were lost men. Strangers surrounded me.
> No tried values existed now.[24]

This sense of displacement prevails in the poems of the immediate post-
war period. In 'The Estrangement' the poet is 'a soul grown strange in
France', moving like a sleepwalker through a 'grim No Man's Land'; in
'Blindfold' he is 'like an exile'; and in 'Death of Childhood Beliefs' he asks,
'How shall I return and how / Look once more on those old places!'

Blunden's marriage to Mary renewed his close contact with country life.
Her close-knit family and their home in Cheveley, near Newmarket,
brought him relief from his recent experiences: 'Anything more remote
from the army life in which I had been submerged for some years could not
be imagined than that almost silent snowy road, the park wall, the dull
inn, the rows of brick cottages without a shellhole in their roofs or in their
gardens, the church and the clockface on the tower.'[25] This sense of release
found expression in his poetry: he could claim in 'The Forest' that it was
still possible to take pleasure in the wood because it reminded him of 'a
green shade of Aveluy Wood' where he found a temporary respite from the
war:

> refreshed thence and whole
> I went to live or die, and five years are flown,
> But not till now was I with the woods again alone.

'The Forest' suggests that with the help of the benevolent power of
nature Blunden may be able to shake off or at least come to terms with his
experiences; but there was another, disquieting note in his poetry that

[23] *The Poet Speaks: interviews with contemporary poets*, edited by Peter Orr, London,
Routledge and Kegan Paul, 1966, p. 36.
[24] 'Aftertones', *The Mind's Eye*, p. 34.
[25] Quoted in *Edmund Blunden*, p. 84.

qualified this optimism. Even before the war Blunden had recognised a terrible aspect to nature – the calamities that befall the farmer in 'The Barn'– and his service in France intensified this awareness. This surely qualifies Leavis' observation that Blunden was trying to create a pastoral world apart from adult distresses and memories of war, when a close examination of some of his rural poems shows that they have been infiltrated by those very elements. Leavis saw Blunden's inclusion of a 'tooth and claw' element in his idyllic world as an imaginative symbol of man's self-torn existence and the poet's awareness of it, an accurate comment if we remember that this recognition was based on something as tangible and as real as Blunden's recent experiences.

Undertones of war are detectable in several of Blunden's poems of 1919. 'Malefactors' describes how slaughtered foxes and stoats, 'Clutched to your clumsy gibbet, shrink to shapeless orts' (perhaps suggestive of dead soldiers rotting on barbed wire), have their revenge on their assassin, the miller, whose business has been abandoned. Blunden asks:

> Felons of fur and feather, can
>   There lurk some crime in man,
>
> In man your executioner,
> Whom here Fate's cudgel battered down?

In 'The Pike' the weir has 'bastions' (a military term for fortifications), and its apparent peace is destroyed by the fish's sudden offensive. (The pike was a creature of fearful fascination for Blunden: in *Undertones of War* he remembers: 'one of my instinctive terrors in my early life had been the sudden sight of a great fish lurking'; and later he writes of seeing one in the canal at Givenchy – an incident he celebrated in 'War Autobiography': 'By the shrapnelled lock I'd prowl /To see below the proud pike doze.'[26]) The wind in 'Spring Night' blows 'So mad ... so truceless and so grim, /As if day's host of flowers were a moment's whim.' – 'Truceless' forcibly reminding us of the war. In 'Perch-Fishing' the successful catch of the 'ogling hunchbacked perch with needled fin' is qualified by Blunden's compassion for the bereft mate, thinking of 'a thousand things the whole year through they did together, never more to do'. And in a later poem, 'Water Moment', published in *To Nature* in June 1923, the murderous eel strikes with the deadly accuracy of a sniper's bullet. The images of sudden violence and terror in these poems are not only revelations of the concealed powers of destruction in nature but also of the vulnerability of the mind to the war's most lasting effect, 'its depth of ironic cruelty'.[27]

Perhaps the most revealing poem of this period is 'The Veteran'. Ostensibly a portrait of his former and much-admired colonel, G.H. Harrison, it

[26] Op. cit., p. 31.
[27] Ibid., p. 266.

is also about Blunden and the problems he faced after the termination of his military service. Although Harrison appears to be contented with his country farm retirement, there is an undertow of uneasiness; his garden has been invaded by memories of the war. Each image of security contains a reminder of the cost at which it has been achieved, and the final lines of the poem bring not serenity but disquiet:

> And if sleep seem unsound,
> And set old bugles pealing through the dark,
> Waked on the instant, he but wakes to hark
> His bellman cockerel crying the first round.

Blunden's first post-Armistice war poems (probably written in 1920-1921 – some appeared in periodicals during that time) were published in April 1922 in *The Shepherd*, subtitled *Poems of peace and war*. The substantial number of war poems in this volume demonstrates Blunden's growing desire or need to confront his war experiences, an exercise he was able to attempt as time distanced him from the events involved. (It may also owe something to his fear of being dismissed as a Georgian poet, proficient only when, as he complained to Sassoon, 'apostrophising a turnip'.[28]) These poems are collected in the 'Impacts of War' section, the title of which reflects that it is only with these early post-war poems that the full impact of the war begins to make itself felt on his consciousness.

The war poems in *The Shepherd* introduce a major theme in Blunden's war writings: war-hauntedness. Sassoon maintained that Blunden was the poet of the war most lastingly obsessed by it, and the beginnings of this obsession – characterised by guilt at having survived, and the consequent need to remember those who died – are revealed in these poems.[29] 'Behind the Line' exhorts the poet to forget the war; but is of no use:

> And still you wander muttering on
> Over the shades of shadows gone.

In 'The Avenue' the poet is distracted from his search for beauty by the image of a colonnade of trees, which reminds him of the endless marches in France down similar roads. It is a memory that will forever intrude upon his poetic vocation:

> The trees hide backwards in the mist, the men
> Are lying in their thankless graves agen,
> And I a stranger in my home pass by
> To seek and serve the beauty that must die.

[28] Quoted in *Edmund Blunden*, p. 130.
[29] See Jon Silkin, *Out of Battle: the poetry of the Great War*, London, OUP, 1972, p. 102.

Guilt at having survived when so many are buried in 'thankless graves' is articulated in 'War Autobiography':

> Then down and down I sank from joy
> To shrivelled age, though scarce a boy,
> And knew for all my fear to die
> That I with those lost friends should lie.

And in 'Reunion in War':

> Why slept not I in Flanders clay
> With all the murdered men.

Desmond Graham acutely observes: 'Blunden's state of mind and not the war itself is the [poems'] subject. He would honestly show us where he is, without making any attempt to help or direct us across the gap in experience. Furthermore, the art is less threatened than the mind that makes it. The act of making verse has brought simple, affirmative rhythms which, even when troubled, retain a cadence we can enjoy.'[30] '1916 seen from 1920', however, brings us to the brink of crossing that gap.

We see the poet in 1921, 'grown old before my day', remembering his experiences in 1916, when he was a new arrival in France and it was still possible to 'snatch long moments from the grudging wars'. The war has yet to destroy his peace of mind or his faith in nature:

> then in warm swoon
> The sun hushed all but the cool orchard plots,
> We crept in the tall grass and slept till noon.

But the serenity of these final lines is disturbed by the knowledge that the morning had seen 'whining shots/Spun from the wrangling wire', and the awareness that the afternoon may bring the experience of war.

In the last war poem in *The Shepherd*, 'Third Ypres', Blunden crosses the gap in experience. None of his previous pieces could have prepared the reader, or indeed the poet, for such an ambitious piece. The only other war-descriptive poem in *The Shepherd* is the brief lyric 'A Farm in Zillebeke', and Blunden probably realised that this form was inadequate for the kind of battle experience he wished to convey; an intention he was quite clear about, describing 'Third Ypres' in the preliminary to *Undertones of War* as 'one of his most comprehensive and particular attempts to render war experience poetically.'[31] It is also obvious from another poem

---

[30] Desmond Graham, *The Truth of War: Owen, Blunden, Rosenberg*, Manchester, Carcanet, p. 84. This work contains the best close reading of Blunden's war poems, although it only covers those in the 'Supplement' to *Undertones of War* in any depth.

[31] Op. cit., p. viii.

in *The Shepherd*, 'A Troubled Spirit', which attempts a cosmic overview of events, that he was looking for a more expansive approach to his experiences.

Barry Webb remarks that Blunden had intended to record his experiences in an extended poem, 'recollected in tranquillity', with Wordsworth's 'Prelude' as his model, 'feeling that the elusive suggestiveness of verse would be more suitable than the starker statements of prose, and that "Third Ypres" is a kind of first draft.'[32] In fact the poetic version of the battle is rather more agitated and immediate than the prose one, with a wider emotional and technical response to the event than the subdued objective tone used in *Undertones of War* – more obviously a work 'recollected in tranquillity'.

The Third Battle of Ypres, begun on 31 July 1917, was intended to launch a campaign to drive back the German Army fifteen miles beyond Ypres within the first eight days, and then break their hold on the Western Front within six months. Bad weather and worse planning achieved an advance of seven miles, the capture of the devastated village of Passchendaele, and a loss of 256,000 British soldiers. Blunden's poem, subtitled 'A Reminiscence', is a microcosm of this operation, featuring the involvement of his battalion from early morning on 31 July to midnight on 2 August.

Using his own experience of a mind burdened almost beyond the point of human endurance, Blunden reveals the besieged mentality of the soldier who has survived for any length of time at the front. And in the poem's emotional trajectory from optimism to despair, he traces the course of the war itself: from the uplift of the first word, 'Triumph!' – an 'extravagant' hope soon disabused by events – to the irony of its last imperative, 'Relieve!' – by which time any survivors are too damaged, mentally and perhaps physically, to enjoy the fruits of such a command.

Paralleling the theme of the fate of the individual in war is that of the fate of the countryside. The poem opens with an irreconcilable contrast between nature and war:

> Triumph! how strange, how strong had triumph come
> On weary hate of foul and endless war,
> When from its grey gravecloths awoke anew
> The summer day.

Later Blunden uses the pastoral image of a ploughman, emphasising the proper use of the land, to point up its present abuse:

> Dizzy we pass the mule-strewn track where once
> The ploughman whistled as he loosed his team;
> And where he turned home-hungry on the road
> The leaning pollard marks us hungrier still.

[32] Op. cit., p. 90.

The conflict reaches some sort of individual resolution at the climax of the poem when, driven almost insane by the spectacle of his mangled companions, the poet is saved by the incongruous appearance of some of nature's gentlest creations:

> And while I squeak and gibber over you,
> Out of the wreck a score of field-mice nimble,
> And tame and curious look about them. (These
> Calmed, on these depended my salvation.)

(Blunden would never have utilised Isaac Rosenberg's sanative recourse: the 'droll rat' in 'Break of Day in the Trenches'.)

The poem ends with an infernal vision of the countryside forever 'amuck with murder, / Each moment puffed into a year with death'; a vision beyond reality, and perhaps beyond exorcism.

> But who with what command can now relieve
> The dead men from that chaos, or my soul?

In 'Third Ypres' Blunden retains his usual archaic diction and phrasing, but combines this with colloquial speech and contemporary language to communicate a sense of tension and danger. This greater variety of 'voices' and his use of blank verse – offering none of the verbal harmony of his earlier war poetry – ensures that 'Third Ypres' remains a disturbing and painful poem.

The first war poem in *The Shepherd*, '11th R.S.R.', is a tribute to Blunden's old battalion and a testament to their continued power over his emotions:

> Your faith still routs my dread,
> Your past and future are my parapet.

But this is not enough to keep the demons at bay:

> What mercy is it I should live and move,
> If haunted by war's agony.

Blunden's agony, exacerbated by problems with his marriage, was becoming apparent to his friends. Acknowledging that he was 'in bad health, which seemed to me to be gaining ground', he allowed himself to be persuaded to take a voyage in December 1921 to Bahia Blanca, Argentina, on the cargo ship S.S. *Trefusis*, to 'do something to take away the taste of Stuff Trench.'[33]

---

[33] Edmund Blunden, *The Bonadventure: a random journal of an Atlantic holiday*, London, Cobden-Sanderson, p. 7; ibid., p. 9.

As a remedy, the voyage was a failure. He had war nightmares of his company halted in the open waiting for a relief that never came. A glass of lime juice reminded him of the taste of trench lemonade; 'and there goes the foolish heart back to Flanders. Even here, in the Atlantic's healthy blue, I am at the mercy of a coincidence in lime juice.'[34] Commissioned to write a travel book during the voyage (published as *The Bonadventure* in December 1922), Blunden also wrote 'A Summer's Fancy', a long, fiction-alised account of his pre-war and wartime life in rhyme royal, the traditional form for such narratives. Revised and published in November 1930, the poem may represent another attempt to describe the war on a wider poetic canvas than usual. But there is an uninspired quality about the poem (the pastoral, on this occasion, seems to have constrained Blunden's imagination), which would suggest that having been unable to escape his memories – 'still dreams came; the war continued' – he used the act of writing the poem as a means of harnessing them.[35]

After his return from the voyage, Blunden devoted himself to work: reviewing, journalism, editing (the work of Christopher Smart and more John Clare), and poetry. 'Rural Economy (1917)', 'The Aftermath', 'The Brook', 'The Self-Imprisoned', and 'The Still Hour', published in *To Nature* in June 1923, are all about the war; the first directly so (reprinted, like 'Third Ypres', in *Undertones of War*), the latter elaborating on the themes of war-hauntedness and alienation:

> Time has healed the wound, they say,
> Gone's the weeping and the rain;
> Yet you and I suspect, the day
> Will never be the same again.
> 'The Aftermath'

To Nature is one of Blunden's most melancholy volumes, with many of the poems featuring a figure no longer comfortable with either nature or himself. This is also the background to 'Old Homes' (not reprinted here), originally published in June 1922, a celebration of his childhood in Yald-ing, memories of which had sustained him throughout the war and its aftermath:

> O happiest village! how I turned to you
> Beyond estranging years that cloaked my view
> With all the wintriness of fear and strain;
> I turned to you, I never turned in vain.

Memories, or 'visions', of childhood continue to be 'a herb of grace to keep the will from madding', and the poem concludes with the claim that 'in

[34] Ibid., p. 65.
[35] Ibid., p. 42.

16

your pastoral still my life has rest.'[36] This obsession with the past, and the apparent lack of faith in the present, may help to explain why Blunden was so eager to accept the offer of a three-year tenure as Professor of English at Tokyo University. Other contributory factors undoubtedly were financial necessity, a long-held desire to see Japan, and perhaps the need to escape from the pain of his failing marriage. He sailed for Japan in March 1924, where, after a short period of isolation and unhappiness, he began to feel at ease and able to write – the 'Preliminary' in the second edition of *Undertones of War*, published in March 1929, is dated 1924.

Blunden's first collection from Japan, published in a limited edition in June 1925 as *Masks of Time*, was a selection of 'principally meditative' pieces, many of them new war poems.[37] The war poems all found their way into the poetical supplement to *Undertones of War*; the pastoral poems mostly were reprinted in January 1926 in *English Poems*. More than in any other collection, the balancing of Blunden's principal poetic concerns, pastoralism and war – the masks of time of the title – is achieved to the most dramatic effect. Barry Webb remarks: 'the distance from England sharpened the "strange perspective" [the title of a poem in the collection] of his vision of melancholic undertones of country life, which was becoming established as the Blunden voice.'[38] This is equally true of the war poems, and *Masks of Time* contains some of his most impressive pieces.

One of the pastoral poems in particular exemplifies Blunden's 'strange perspective'. Many critics have commented on the military undertones of 'The Midnight Skaters': the use of the word 'parapet' and the image of death as a machine under the ice. But the poem can also be read as an allegory of Blunden's successful harnessing of his war experiences. Skating is a metaphor for writing, the ice, or 'crystal parapet', symbolises the written word, and the 'secret waters', the intractable memories of war. Because of the ice, the skater can master the danger of the pond; if he acts with courage and sense, safety and sanity can be maintained. Blunden's 'crystal parapet' was, of course, *Undertones of War* with its 'Supplement of Poetical Interpretations and Variations'.

Blunden's prose account of his war experiences was written in a hotel room in Tokyo with the help of a couple of trench maps, but otherwise entirely from memory. This was a conscious attempt on Blunden's part to distance himself from events, which, when it came to writing *Undertones of War*, allowed the undertones of time to add perspective to the narrative. His persona of 'a harmless young shepherd in a soldier's coat' was another distancing device to enable him to confront his memories. He wrote to G.H. Grubb in May 1930: 'In Japan, my sense of loss and eyelessness became stronger, the first year there being of course productive of long periods of

[36] *Poems 1914-30*, pp. 94-98.
[37] Edmund Blunden, *Masks of Time: a new collection of poems principally meditative*, London, Beaumont Press, 1925.
[38] Op. cit., p. 150.

17

loneliness, though later on I discovered many springs of hope and sympathy. I also had some *time* now & then, – & so I began to picture the past as well as I could in words. (I had deliberately left my old notes in England, and wrote without the awkward means of checking my memory, – on the whole, this was probably good luck.)'[39] In 1918 Blunden had attempted an account of his experiences, entitled *De Bello Germanico*, which covered the period from his landing in France to his leaving Richebourg for the Somme in July 1916. It remained unpublished until 1930 (when Blunden gave it to his brother Gilbert who was setting up as a printer) because 'although in its details not much affected by the perplexities of distancing memory, [it] was noisy with a depressing forced gaiety then very much the rage.'[40] In fact it is an exciting and immediate piece of writing, if without the reflection and subtlety of *Undertones of War*.

In his 'Preliminary' to *Undertones of War* Blunden gives as a reason for writing his memoir that his poetry was unable to incorporate the facts and details of his war experiences in a way that a prose narrative could:

> I have been attempting 'the image and the horror of it', with some other personations, in poetry. Even so, when the main sheaves appeared fine enough to my flattering eye, it was impossible not to look again, and to descry the ground, how thickly and innumerably yet it was strewn with the facts or notions of war experience.
> I must go over the ground again.[41]

The 'sheaves' in question presumably were the war poems in *Masks of Time,* and it was their failure, in Blunden's eyes, to communicate his experiences with the necessary depth that prompted the writing of *Undertones of War*. The realisation that something different was needed had struck Blunden as early as January 1917, when he wrote home: 'I wish I could weave together all the moods and manners that I see out here, and make an epic of the age.'[42] *Undertones of War,* with its 'Supplement of Poetical Interpretations and Variations', was the fulfilment of that desire – the epic of his generation. He told an interviewer that he had always intended that the book be considered as 'a sort of long poem. It varies, of course, in topics, but the uniting argument, if there is one, is that war is like that and ought not to happen.'[43] And if *Undertones of War* does not fulfil all the criteria for the traditional epic, we should value it no less for that, and remember instead Maurice Bowra's observation: 'Modern war provides no material comparable with that of the *Iliad* or *Henry V*, and the

---

[39] Quoted in Thomas Mallon, *Edmund Blunden*, Boston, Twayne, 1973, pp. 64-65.
[40] *Undertones of War*, p. viii.
[41] Ibid., p. viii.
[42] Quoted in Mallon, p. 67.
[43] *The Poet Speaks*, p. 37.

poets have to take it as they find it. Their record of what they found has its own tragic distinction.'[44]

Although some of the poems in the 'Supplement' had already been written before Blunden began the prose narrative, it is clear from his comments to the interviewer quoted above that he meant them both to be part of the final work. Of the thirty-two poems that comprise the 'Supplement', one is reprinted from *The Shepherd* ('Third Ypres'), one from *To Nature* ('Rural Economy (1917)'), and fifteen from *Masks of Time*. Presumably the remaining poems were composed during and inspired by the writing of *Undertones of War*. The first nineteen poems recreate scenes and events behind the line and in the trenches – the 'poetical interpretations'; the last thirteen portray the memory revisiting those scenes and events – the 'poetical variations'. Because of this difference in theme, I have separated the 'Supplement' into two sections, 'Undertones of War' and 'Delayed Actions'. The former includes two extra poems, 'Premature Rejoicing' and 'Into the Salient', inserted into the original sequence by Blunden in *Poems 1914-1930*; the latter includes 'Return of the Native', added by Blunden to the second edition of *Undertones of War*, published in June 1930 (the first edition was published in November 1928), and two poems from *Near and Far*, 'Inaccessibility in the Battlefield' and 'War's People', published in September 1929 and included in the 'War: Impacts and Delayed Actions' section of *Poems 1914-1930*.[45]

Many of the poems, certainly those in the 'Undertones of War' section, can be related to an incident in the prose narrative. In general, the poems heighten and intensify the subjective aspect of the incident described; while the prose narrative develops the external aspects, expanding upon the action, often in relation to the immediate military situation. The prose account describes the physical context and builds up a coherent succession of incidents to form the narrative; but the necessity of maintaining a coherent narrative diminishes the opportunities of exploring the area of subjective emotions and sensations – an exercise performed by the poems. Blunden suggests in his preface to the second edition of *Undertones of War* that the poems 'supply details and happenings which would have strengthened the prose had I not already been impelled to express them'; but that would have been a different book altogether, even if Blunden had managed to bring it to completion.[46] It could not have been a tale told by 'a harmless young shepherd in a soldier's coat'.

The poems in the 'Undertones of War' section follow the action of the war in twenty-one scenes (nineteen in the original 'Supplement'). Their course traces the chronology of Blunden's experiences at the front from Festubert to Gouzeaucourt; but the pattern is not a simple one. The poems

[44] Maurice Bowra, *Poetry and the First World War*, London, Clarendon Press, 1961, p. 35.

[45] Edmund Blunden, *Near and Far*, London, Cobden-Sanderson, 1929.

[46] Edmund Blunden, *Undertones of War*, London, Cobden-Sanderson, 1929 (second edition), p. vii.

do not record, as shown in the prose narrative, Blunden's progress from innocence to experience; neither is there a logical development in tone of voice or angle of vision. As Desmond Graham observes, within the sequence, and often within the same poem, 'past and present overlap, calm and tension; irony gives way to direct description, the assured lyric voice, to satire.'[47] Indeed there is more variety of form and style in these poems than in the entire corpus of most war poets; and Blunden's range is such that they inevitably include pieces that have something of the characteristics of the work of his most famous contemporaries. In 'The Zonnebeke Road', 'Preparations for Victory', 'Zero', and 'Vlamertinghe: Passing the Chateau, July, 1917' he attains the overwhelming sense of pity that distinguishes Owen's verse: the former two poems match the bleak anguish of 'Exposure'; and the latter two expose romantic rhetoric in a manner comparable to 'Greater Love' and 'Insensibility'. 'Concert Party: Busseboom', 'The Welcome', and 'Pillbox' have something of Sassoon's ironic tone and colloquial manner, the former poem in particular employing a *dénouement* as devastating as anything in Sassoon:

> While men in the tunnels below Larch Wood
> Were kicking men to death.

But perhaps the poet Blunden shares most with is Ivor Gurney, in poems like 'At Senlis Once', 'Trench Raid near Hooge', and 'Battalion in Rest'. Both have an intense appreciation of the countryside, of France as well as England, and both have a keen sense of place. Many of their poems refer to particular places, which, in the case of those less famous than the Somme, Ypres and Passchendaele, may have no meaning for us, but are invested by their poetry with an almost legendary quality.

A rationale for the sequence of the poems in the 'Supplement' can be found in *Undertones of War,* where Blunden observes: 'a peculiar difficulty would exist for the artist to select the sights, faces, words, incidents which characterized the time. The art is rather to collect them, in their original form of incoherence.'[48] In its shifts of mood and accent, the whole sequence, despite its chronological sequence, does reproduce this 'original form of incoherence' in that it reflects the arbitrary and bewildering changes in the fortunes of war as experienced both by the soldier and the poet – as he seeks ways of articulating what is perhaps beyond expression:

> All the same, it's a shade too soon
> For you to scribble rhymes
> In your army book
> About those times;

---

[47] Op. cit., p. 111.
[48] Op. cit., p. 194.

Take another look;
That's where the difficulty is, over there.
'Premature Rejoicing'

Although the sequence deals, as elsewhere in his poetry, with the destructive effect of war on nature – 'A House in Festubert', 'Two Voices', 'Rural Economy (1917)' – Blunden is as concerned to communicate the destructive effect of the war on the men who fought it – 'Escape', 'Battalion in Rest', and 'Pillbox'. His achievement in this regard was succinctly expressed by Blunden himself in his observations on Gurney: 'He described the life of the infantryman ... in a series of subtle reminiscence, catching many details and tones which had combined in the quality of seasons and moments, anguish and relief never again to occur.'[49]

The last poem in the 'Undertones of War' section, 'Gouzeaucourt: the Deceitful Calm', recounts Blunden's departure from the front line, and his subsequent guilt at leaving his comrades behind to face the next onslaught of action:

There it was, my dears, that I departed,
Scarce a plainer traitor ever! There too
    Many of you soon paid for
    That false mildness.

The remaining poems in the 'Supplement', collected here in the 'Delayed Actions' section, take up and expand upon this sense of guilt, anticipated by Blunden in his use of the Bunyan epigraph to *Undertones of War*: 'Yea, how they set themselves in battle-array I shall remember to my dying day.'[50] These are poems of introspection, which record the effects of the war, principally on the mind of the poet – several of them are cast in the form of the poet in conversation with his younger self; and of remembrance, which celebrate and commemorate the companionship of his fellow officers and men.

As one who survived, Blunden assumed the responsibility of preserving the memory of those who were dead – a charge made more urgent by his fear that these deaths were not only in vain but also forgotten. This feeling of futility is most powerfully expressed in 'II Peter, ii, 22', which echoes the Biblical proverb – 'The dog is turned to his own vomit; and the sow that was washed to her wallowing in the mire' – images of rancid pastoralism:

And Quarrel with her hissing tongue
And hen's eyes gobble gross along

---

[49] *Poems by Ivor Gurney*, p. 13.
[50] Op. cit., p. [ix].

> To snap that prey
> That marched away
> To save her carcass, better hung.

Such sarcasm is more typical of Sassoon, and the prevailing mood else-where is one of poignancy. Blunden largely eschews even his characteristic sense of irony, other than in 'The Prophet', which contrasts the description of Flanders taken from a post-Waterloo guide book with a description taken from a post-First World War source – Blunden's own experience; and in 'Trench Nomenclature', which similarly contrasts the soldiers' naming of trenches with the reality they represented.

A number of the poems – 'La Quinque Road', 'The Ancre at Hamel: Afterwards', 'Another Journey from Bethune to Cuinchy', 'Flanders Now', and 'Return of the Native' – were inspired by visits to old battlefields, where memories of blasted landscapes persist even when the landscapes themselves have returned to normal:

> O road, I know these muttering groups you pass,
> I know your art of turning blood to glass;
> But, I am told, tonight you safely shine
> To trim roofs and cropped fields; the error's mine.
>
> 'La Quinque Rue'

Others are tributes to fellow soldiers; both as a group – 'Their Very Memory', 'Flanders Now', and 'War's People' – and as individuals – 'Rec-ognition' (George Maycock), 'A.G.A.V.' (Arnold Vidler), and 'An Infantryman' (James Cassels). All the poems in this section discuss, and at the same time demonstrate, the ineluctable pull of the past, which binds the poet not only with memories of fear but also with ties of love. This contradiction is most movingly expressed in 'The Watchers', but is more eloquently examined in 'On Reading that the Rebuilding of Ypres Ap-proached Completion', where Blunden's recovery of the past carries with it the recognition that the past involved suffering and pain:

> But my danger lies even here, even now worn weak and nerveless
> I go drooping,
> Heavy-headed, and would sleep thus lulled with your love's fulness,
> Sharply awake me
> With fierce words, and as the fangs of bayonets in the frozen saps,
> Simple as the fact that you must kill, or go for rations,
> As clear as morning blue, as red and grotesque as the open mouths
> Of winter corpses.

Undertones of War, with its 'Supplement', represents Blunden's most ambitious and comprehensive attempt to express his experience of war.

The perspective of time which allowed him to make this attempt also demonstrated how unassuagable the experience had become. The act of remembering, and of committing those memories to paper, was not the act of absolution he had anticipated. As Desmond Graham observes: 'Too much had been aroused for personal exorcism to be sufficient or possible. Too many deaths were still felt for a memorial tribute to set matters to rest.'[51]

In the summer of 1929, two years after his return from Japan and almost a year after the publication of *Undertones of War*, Blunden revisited Ypres and recorded what he found there in 'The Return of the Native', a poem whose serenity suggests the laying at last of war's ghosts:

> The old law here
> Had come again with peasant tread to claim
> So full and unabated property
> That not one mark of a mad occupation
> Might be conceived.

But for Blunden the landscape is still charged with violent and tragic memories. As the title suggests – making ironic use of Hardy's title while deploying a Hardyesque kind of irony – he remains an exile to peace and his former life as much as he remains a native of Ypres and the war. Although the last lines of the poem move towards resolution, it remains finally out of reach, obstructed by memories of the dead, 'now incapable to stir a weed or moth.' (This almost animate ability of the past to confound the present is also expressed allegorically in 'Inaccessibility on the Battlefield', where the blasted landscape consistently denies access to the oases of rural beauty.)

'Return of the Native', added by Blunden to the second edition of *Undertones of War*, sets the tone for many of the poems that followed. Although he continued to work on many projects unconnected to the war, the war remained a crucial influence on his poetry; 'The Study' depicts him sitting 'penning plans of dead affairs', and 'Chances of Remembrance' acknowledges that the past, 'a dull brown thicket', will continue to invade the present:

> My thin blood will not wash out,
> My purple brambles will mantle you about,
> My thorny claspings pierce
> Into your verse.

Feelings of being exiled from his former life and disabled in his present one are articulated in several poems of the late nineteen-twenties, col-

[51] Op. cit., p. 85.

lected here in the section 'Experience and Soliloquy'. 'The Crown Inn', 'Old Pleasures Deserted', and 'The Complaint' all feature the poet returning to his former rural haunts, only to find the old ease now gone. And although he continues to be grateful for the consolations of nature and beauty, he can no longer trust them: 'Rue de Bois' and 'In Wiltshire', which begin as celebrations of the countryside, finally only bring memories of the past. This ironic inability to enjoy the scenes that comforted him in war now they have returned to their peaceful state is Blunden's special pain; so much so that 'Warning to Troops' advises a future generation of soldiers to reject the comfort of nature because it makes reality too hard to bear:

> Double not thy war.
> Shun all such sweet prelusion. March, sing, roar,
> Lest perilous silence gnaw thee evermore.

This extremely dark vision is not sustained, and poems like 'Values', 'Report on Experience', and 'The Sunlit Vale' while accepting the reality of a bleaker side to existence also acknowledge the need to have faith in the healing power of nature. In 'Values' Blunden takes an objective view of his past suffering, recognizing that his experiences have taught him that 'Raindrops may murder, lightning may caress.' The poem ends on a note of affirmation:

> From love's wide-flowering mountain-side I chose
> This sprig of green, in which an angel shows.

'Report on Experience', after showing the discrepancy between what formerly was thought true and what experience has revealed, ends on a more tenuous note of affirmation; that we live in an ambiguous world presided over by a distant deity:

> Say what you will, our God sees how they run,
> These disillusions are curious proving
> That the less humanity and will go on loving;
> Over there are faith, life, virtue in the sun.

Over there, but not here? Virtues may exist, but only as idealized abstractions. According to Jon Silkin, Blunden 'tentatively confirmed in conversation that "The Sunlit Vale" glosses on "Report on Experience" ':[52]

> I saw the sunlit vale, and the pastoral fairy-tale;
> The sweet and bitter scent of the may drifted by;
> And never have I seen such a bright bewildering green,

---

[52] Op. cit., p. 120.

But it looked like a lie
Like a kindly meant lie.

A belief in nature as a permanent source of goodness cannot be sustained; the darker side of life has undermined such a conviction. As Silkin remarks: 'The pastoral framework has been shattered by contemporary experience. Nature may be consolatory now, but she is no longer man's preceptress.'[53]

One constant, however, remained. The 'sprig of green' in 'Values', despite its horticultural associations, does not necessarily refer to the consolatory power of nature. Given the poem's title, it could be a symbol for a 'value' that never faded: the love of comrades both alive, as in 'On the Portrait of a Colonel: G.H.H.', and dead. The preservation of the memories of his dead companions especially exercised Blunden's concern, assuming the character of a religious conviction. Hence his outrage at the publication, in November 1929, of Robert Graves' *Good-bye to All That*, which he felt to be 'ugly and untruthful', a distortion little short of heresy.[54] Attempts to forget, or in Graves' case reject, the past were a betrayal; but perhaps what affected Blunden most was that Graves could say 'good-bye to all that', while he 'seemed to [have undertaken] a burden for life during the War of 1914-1918.'[55] The burden at times might seem too heavy, but evasion was unthinkable:

Accept that when the past has beckoned,
There is no help; all else comes second;
Agree, the only way to live
Is not to dissect existence.

'In My Time'

The act of communion with the past brought war dreams of an almost visionary nature: in an undated manuscript, written in Hong Kong sometime between 1953 and 1964, Blunden noted: 'I was looking out the window, high over the square; and others were. On a sudden cords or coils of purple or blue-grey were there on the blue sky, and coming down to our world; and beauty mixed with terror was my impression.'[56] In 1964 he wrote to Laurence Whistler referring to 'that Somme battle which I revisited last night to the last coil of barbed wire, but before I slept.'[57] Actual visits to the battlefields and cemeteries (commemorated in such poems as 'The Memorial', 'From Age to Age', 'At Rugmer', and 'War Cemetery'), both in private and in his official capacity from 1936 as adviser

[53] Ibid., p. 120.
[54] Robert Graves, *Good-bye to All That*, London, Jonathan Cape, 1929; quoted in *Edmund Blunden*, p. 170.
[55] Edmund Blunden, *Cricket Country,* London, Collins, 1944, p. 38.
[56] Quoted in Mallon, p. 62.

to the Imperial War Graves Commission, could only have served to feed such nightmares.

Memories were also kept alive by his regular attendance of the annual Southdown Battalion Reunion, of which his idealised essay about one such occasion, published in June 1932, is appropriately entitled *Fall In, Ghosts*. Blunden's annual reunion poems, even as late as 1938, are generally light-hearted, as befits the occasion. His essay similarly concentrates on the comradeship that motivates such meetings, although he is careful to sound a few notes of caution; an acknowledgement that the reunion 'is our quaint attempt to catch a falling star', and a warning against 'the rhapsodical touch in our reason for bring here.'[58]

The reunion poems and the essay celebrate the 'mystery ... the misery and the dignity [that] reside in the word "the battalion". The future cannot rival that attraction. They, we, are years behind even the present, and minor reservations and limitations of date, place and contract yield to the one strong retrospective migratory devotion.'[59] This is also the theme of several poems in the 'Can You Remember?' section: 'Fancy and Memory', 'November 1, 1931', 'Unlucky Allusions', 'The Lost Battalion', 'At Rugmer', 'In My Time', 'Cabaret Tune', and 'Can You Remember?'; poems which examine war-hauntedness as much as they express it. The feeling of personal guilt in these poems is less acute than in Blunden's earlier work; there is a sense that his experience is its own validation, even if he did survive. In 'At Rugmer' he is reminded by the falling leaves of autumn that once 'our season seemed /At any second closing'; he continues, 'So, we were wrong.' But instead of prompting guilt, this realization brings acceptance:

> But we have lived this landscape,
> And have an understanding with these shades.

This more equable, balanced frame of mind may partly be due to his divorce from Mary in February 1931, and his introduction to Sylva Norman, a journalist and writer, later that year. (They were married in July 1933.) In a letter he wrote to her in March 1932, she appears at the end of the description of a shelled Festubert road:

> And you are come, and there is need of you,
> As much as on that track of blood and dew,
> O you shall conquer, dear, and the weak day
> Shall even yield you grace and roundelay.[60]

---

[57] Quoted in *Edmund Blunden*, p. 98.
[58] Op. cit., p. 248; ibid., p. 250.
[59] Ibid., p. 257.
[60] Quoted in *Edmund Blunden*, p. 201.

Sylva's importance as an influence on Blunden to rival the war is most clearly seen in their joint literary venture, a novel, *We'll Shift Our Ground*, based on a visit in summer 1932 to the battlefields. A facetious work, which reads like an extended private lovers' joke, it is most interesting for the dearth of Blunden's customary war reminiscences; an absence he tacitly acknowledges at one point: 'The road was free and open, and crossed the down with great purity of design; it was not the old, sly and blood-stained vision, but he had better picture it as it had grown to be.'[61]

That the past could still disorientate Blunden is demonstrated by poems like 'November 1, 1931', 'The Lost Battalion', and 'Fancy and Memory', where 'memory', although preferred to 'fancy', can prove to be unreliable, bringing both happy and unhappy memories:

> Music she has that richly speaks her mind;
> So saying, she with Orpheus vies; I hear,
> And Flemish church-tower vanes glint in the wind
> And man and horse and crow again live near, –
> Man, horse, and guns and mines and tanks renew
> Daybreak's demented duel – Memory, *et tu?*

But there is a greater sense in the poems of this period that the experience of war has been assimilated – in 'Cabaret Tune' he accepts that he will be moving 'for ever between "Now and Then" ' – although this is not a matter for complacency. The last line of 'From Age to Age' may aver that 'life's too short for wondering, too aflame for weeping', but the clipped tone of the poem indicates that this is not Blunden's attitude. The poem laments the failure of memorials and cemeteries, 'history's marble eyes', to remind the world of the dead; a theme explored by other poems in this section: 'The Memorial 1914-1918', 'Inscribed in War Books', 'Some Talk of Peace', and 'War Cemetery'. Blunden is particularly bitter in 'The Memorial 1914-1918' and 'War Cemetery', an emotion fuelled by his fear not only that the dead are being forgotten but also by his suspicion that such forgetfuless may become dangerous. Echoing 'The Return of the Native', in 'The Branch Line' a steam train again reminds Blunden of the war; but whereas the earlier poem ended on a note of tentative resolution, the later one concludes with the horrified thought, 'and should that come again.' The fear of another war is also present in 'Anti-Basilisk', which enacts the delusion that wars can be won, if the trick can be found, and in 'On a Picture by Dürer' which warns that if man cannot learn from history, he is doomed to repeat himself.

As the threat of war grew steadily throughout the nineteen-thirties, so did Blunden's denials of its possibility; a position that became increasingly difficult to maintain, and which led him to being accused of having

[61] Edmund Blunden and Sylva Norman, *We'll Shift our Ground: or Two on a Tour*, London, Cobden-Sanderson, 1933, p. 182.

sympathy with a number of extreme political opinions, although he was only ever motivated by the desire to avoid another war. *An Elegy and other Poems*, published in November 1937 (from which many of the poems in this section are taken), reflects this mood of tension and anxiety.[62] Without actually articulating the fear of future conflict, this clearly is the dynamic of poems like 'Recurrence' and 'Stanzas: Midsummer, 1937', and of the poems that revisit scenes of war in the 'Echoes from the Great War' section.

These poems are about the recovery of the past, both in theory and practice, with the uncertainty of the poems from *An Elegy and other Poems* giving way to the nostalgia of the poems taken from Blunden's own 'Echoes from the Great War' section, published in June 1941 in *Poems 1930-1940*.[63] Many of these are set in 1916 before the full horror of the war became apparent; when it was still possible to find an oasis of calm and natural beauty out of the front line: 'To walk among the gun-fogged dwellings /And keep in touch with something Kind' ('Ruins'). 1916 was a seminal period for Blunden and one that he returned to with frequency. In his introduction to *Poems by Ivor Gurney: principally selected from unpublished manuscripts*, published in September 1954, he sees this time also as a crucial one for Gurney, and his comments consequently are self-revelatory:

> Those of us who were in that region [between Brumentières and Béthune] in the summer of 1916 remember, apart from the intervals of violent and profitless battle in the trench zone, the inexpressible loveliness and lure of the passing hour. The country close to the line was still very little harmed; its husbandry remained quietly perfect; its substantial towns, villages, lonely corners, field-side shrines, avenues, villas, brooks and canals, beneath blue and white skies, were peace itself – and more than common peace to those who found themselves alive and respited for a space .... Add to this that Gurney ... was with men of his own shire, in whom a like tradition and similar ability were personified, and we may see how this passage of his life as a soldier became a deep delight to him. When we observe that with it were mingled the extreme horror and futility of his battlefield days and nights, we apprehend the whole force of the period as it fastened on his imagination; and this also became even a tyranny over his later poetry.[64]

Blunden visited Gurney at Dartford Asylum, where he was incarcerated, probably sometime in the late nineteen-twenties, a meeting which partly inspired the poem 'Mental Hospital'. In his copy of *Poems by Ivor Gurney*

---

[62] Edmund Blunden, *An Elegy and other Poems*, London, Cobden-Sanderson, 1937.

[63] Edmund Blunden, *Poems 1930-1940*, London, Macmillan, 1940.

[64] Op. cit., p. 11.

he wrote: 'I see him yet, and hear him too – singing and playing to a naked frosty sky.'[65]

A comparison of Blunden's earlier poem '1916 seen from 1921' with 'Near Albert-sur-Ancre', also set in 1916, reveals a diminution in urgency and complexity. Similarly, 'From the Battle Zone' is melancholic, but without the pathos of 'A House in Festubert'. 1916 seen from the late nineteen-thirties is a less focused and more rose-tinted vision than 1916 seen from the early nineteen-twenties. There is a sense with these later poems that Blunden was restricting himself to a response he felt capable of controlling amd interpreting, and consequently they have little of the ambition and range of his earlier poems, especially those from *Undertones of War*. Previously Blunden had attempted to make the reader live his experiences and the varieties of response they incurred; in these later poems he seems content to describe his emotions and the incidents in which he was involved, although he ruefully acknowledges in 'Rhymes on Bethune': 'I cannot see them now, I grieve /To fail in this.' With the passage of time the echoes from the Great War inevitably have become fainter and less dissonant. Also diminished is the tension between the pastoral ideal and the reality of war, both in terms of language and concept. It is almost as if the war itself has become the ideal: it is not 'skinny trees /And unmossed clay' by which Blunden chooses to remember Martinsart Wood, but its 'green grace':

> Thus to me in the vale of years
>   Holy almost and serene
> Martinsart Wood appears.
>   May you be fresh and green,
> Dear coppice, when Doomsday nears!

But the 'Doomsday' of Martinsart Wood was taking tangible shape beyond that of a literary image and it was a reality Blunden could no longer avoid.

In 1938 Blunden made what was to be his last visit to France before the outbreak of war, a bitter-sweet experience as recorded in the poems 'In West Flanders' and 'Travellers 193-'. Although the threat of war is mentioned in neither poem, it is present in both: in the lines 'The autumn evening now impending /Changes the painted lake we found' in 'In West Flanders', and in 'I feel at once deep joy and trouble, /And winds blowing each separate way' in 'Travellers193-'. Blunden also visited Germany four times between August 1935 and 1939, casting himself in the role of a cultural ambassador, and in the poems 'About These Germans' and 'A Window in Germany: August 1939' he defended what he saw as the basic goodness of the German people. (He did the same for the Japanese in 'In the Margin'.) These visits attracted considerable controversy, not least

---

[65] Quoted in *Edmund Blunden*, p. 290.

among Blunden's friends, but his desparate desire to avoid another war led to such desperate remedies, especially as all other efforts appeared to have failed.

He was particularly tormented by the thought, expressed in 'To W.O. and his Kind', 'War Talk: Winter 1938', and 'To the Southdowns: At the yearly Reunion, 1939', that he and his generation had failed to convince the next generation – 'The Same Englishmen' – of the horror and futility of war, and to 'slow /Their haste to reach a wasteful end.' This perceived failure led Blunden to look for a political solution, which accounts for 'Exorcized', written in response to the Munich agreement of September 1938. The poem's misguided trust in appeasement and its wayward inclusion of Hitler and Mussolini among 'the generous, selfless, wise' only emphasize his despair at the thought of another war, memories of which came flooding back with renewed force. Having believed that he had made a separate peace with the past, the threat of war summoned ghosts he thought had been laid to rest:

> I yield; I can no other; habit looks
> Stronger again. Adieu, return, my ghost!
> 'At My Writing Desk'

Blunden's faith in the Munich agreement informs both 'The Sum of All', with its faith in the 'enchanting haunting fanciful music of life', and 'A Window in Germany: August 1939', which celebrates a landscape comparable to an 'English casual scene ... /Of rural mastery, and of rural ease', watched over by 'far-sundered ghosts, /To whom my ways mean something'. But within the month Blunden saw the collapse of all his hopes:

> ... [']The placid length
> Of the crystal lake lies like a war-god's shield,
> Fallen for boys to find while flying kites afield.'
> So even this spring
> I wrote, I started with never a wild surmise
> Near that old frontier. Now the hideous thing
> Is loose again, the ready death-forms rise.
> 'By the Belgian Border'

From 3 September 1939 Blunden began to keep a diary in order to record the progress of the war and his reactions to it. According to Barry Webb: 'Its pages give the clearest picture of Edmund's ambivalent political position and reveal a gradual if reluctant acceptance of the aggressive nature of German intentions.'[66] Through the pages of his diary he began also to relive his experiences in the First World War, prompted by the fact

[66] Op. cit., p. 224.

that almost every day was the anniversary of an earlier action. The diary ends abruptly in mid-1942, partly because Blunden feared that many of the sentiments expressed might put him at risk with the authorities (he was in fact under police surveillance at the beginning of the war for his German sympathies), and partly because he was tired of 'retrospective tunnellings' and felt that he had said all that he wished on 'war rather than this war'.[67] This perhaps explains why so few of his Second World War poems make imaginative use of the First World War. There was also the feeling that the Second World War was not his war: he had made his attempt to prevent its outbreak, and had thus discharged his duty to his dead comrades. His personal resistance to the war effectively ceased when he became a map-reading instructor with an honorary rank of captain in July 1942.

The despair Blunden had felt at the outbreak of war was partially mitigated by his meeting, and subsequent falling in love, with Claire Margaret Poynting in September 1939. He wrote to Sassoon in November 1940: 'If you were to ask how I got through some of the mud and filth and blanks of 1939-40, I should name young Claire Poynting.'[68] Blunden's marriage to Sylva had been platonic for some time, and knowing that he was eager to start a family, she agreed eventually to a divorce. After a lengthy wait, Blunden and Claire were married in May 1945.

Shells by a Stream, published in October 1944, charts his growing love for Claire, which he associates with a renewed belief in the regenerative power of nature.[69] Despite the fact that they were written during a war that had fulfilled his worst fears, there is an optimism to the poems in this collection which had been largely absent from the volumes published in the nineteen-thirties. When the war, either by implication or direct reference, enters the poems, it is not in the form of Blunden's own memories, but rather as part of a shared contemporary response. Even though 'A Survivor From One War Reflects during Another' invokes the First World War, it deals in universalities rather than particulars.

The two Second World War poems included in 'The Next War' section, 'To Wilfred Owen' and 'Darkness', are not taken from Shells by a Stream and share nothing of that volume's buoyancy; but they do both express a tenuous faith in the future, although in the former poem it is based on no good reason, and in the latter it is almost submerged by the horror of the present.

As far as his own happiness was concerned, Blunden's faith in the future was justified. His marriage to Claire brought not only children but also contentment and security. The post-war years also saw a renewed and successful acquaintance with Japan, from December 1947 to May 1950, as

---

[67] Quoted in ibid., p. 228.
[68] Quoted in ibid., p. 221.
[69] Edmund Blunden, Shells by a Stream, London, Macmillan, 1944.

a roving cultural ambassador, and a longer period in Hong Kong, from September 1953 to May 1964, as Professor of English at the University. The later years of his time in Hong Kong were clouded when he began to suffer from depression brought on by ailing health, overwork, and a crisis of confidence in his creative powers. Certainly he wrote less in the years following the Second World War, but the poetry he did publish, principally in the volumes *After the Bombing, Poems of Many Years* (a selected edition with new poems), *Eastward, A Hong Kong House,* and *Eleven Poems,* published in October 1949, March 1950, June 1957, November 1959 and March 1966 respectively, are distinguished by his characteristic persuasive, gentle, and contemplative tone of voice.[70]

Memories of the First World War, distanced by time and event, had become less insistent, although they still had the ability to take him by surprise, if more infrequently than before. In 'The Halted Battalion', written in 1946, 'One hour from far returns', and the memory reminds him that poets, by virtue of their vocation, will always remember:

> We who draw
> Picture and meaning are the dreamless, we
> Are sentinels of time while the rest are free.

A sudden memory from the past prompts other poems in the 'Aftertones of War' section: 'Over the Valley', 'The Little Song', and 'Ancre Sunshine'. The past also steals into poems far removed from the war in circumstance – 'The Hedgehog Killed in the Road', – place – 'At the Great Wall of China', – and time – 'A Swan, A Man'. Some poems are recreations of war scenes: 'Echo of War', 'Ancre, 1916', and 'Armistice: A March'; and others are tributes to old friends: 'Frank Worley, D.C.M., July 1954', '1966: S.S. becomes an Octogenarian', and The Gun in 'Gone'.

Although Blunden has never been defined by the term 'war poet', the war is a defining element in his poetry. In the year before his death he chose 'Can You Remember?' to represent his work in an anthology, because 'my experiences in the First World War have haunted me all my life and for many days I have, it seemed, lived in that world rather than this'.[71] His war experience not only prompted some of his most moving and accomplished poetry, but it also indelibly affected his outlook on life. As Philip Gardner succinctly observes: 'The fragility of nature and human life, which war taught him, only increased his appreciation of their beauty and value; and as they helped to maintain a sense of perspective in wartime,

[70] Edmund Blunden, *After the Bombing,* London, Macmillan, 1949; Edmund Blunden, *Poems of Many Years,* London, Collins, 1957; Edmund Blunden, *Eastward,* Kyoto, 'English Poetry', 1959; Edmund Blunden, *A Hong Kong House,* London, Poetry Book Society, 1959.
[71] *Let the Poet Choose,* edited by James Gibson, London, Harrap, 1973, p. 31.

so wartime itself, recalled in peace, prevented complacency, and brought to Blunden's poetry a bracing tension.'[72]

It was entirely appropriate that his last poem, 'Ancre Sunshine', should have been written on his final visit to France, and that it was a poem about the war.[73] The prophecy he had expressed in the 'Preliminary' to *Undertones of War* had proved clairvoyant:

> A voice, perhaps not my own, answers within me. You will be going over the ground, it says, until that hour when agony's clawed face softens into the smilingness of a young spring day; when ... it shall be the simplest thing to take in your hands the hands of companions like E.W.T., and W.J.C., and A.G.V., in whose recaptured gentleness no sign of death's astonishment or time's separation shall be imaginable.[74]

In one of his last prose pieces, 'Infantryman Passes By', written for the First World War anthology *Promise of Greatness*, published in November 1968, Blunden wrote: 'To try to chronicle the miseries and destructions of the days thus began would be to invite sleepless nights or insane dreams, which have been exorcized, in any event, during the half century.'[75] Perhaps at the end he did manage to say 'good-bye to all that'. Certainly in his last years at Long Melford in Suffolk, a pastoral retreat reminiscent of the villages of his childhood, he seemed less troubled by memories from the past.

He died from a heart attack on 20 July 1974. At the funeral on the 25th, his passing was commemorated by a presence Blunden would have honoured and respected above all others: Private A.E. Beeney, his runner at Ypres and Passchendaele, and one of the last surviving members of 11th Battalion, The Royal Sussex Regiment.

> It seems, as now I wake and brood,
> And know my hour's decrepitude,
> That on some dewy parapet
> The sentry's spirit gazes yet,
> Who will not speak with altered tone
> When I at last am seen and known.
> 'The Watchers'

MARTIN TAYLOR

---

[72] Philip Gardner, 'Edmund Blunden: War Poet', *University of Toronto Quarterly*, Vol. XLII, No. 3, Spring 1973, p. 239.

[73] Published in *Garland*, Cambridge, Golden Head Press, 1968.

[74] Op. cit., p. viii.

[75] Edmund Blunden, 'Infantryman Passes By', *Promise of Greatness: the war of 1914-1918*, edited by George A. Panichas, New York, John Day, 1968.

THE SHEPHERD AT WAR

October 1914

FROM the white cottage on the glimmering wold
That sees the clustering village far away,
And hears no sound of life, the autumn day,
But tread of its own housewife hale and old;
And from the cottage in the fenland hold,
Where ancient gravel-pits are now the prey
Of slothful deeps and sedges withering gray;
And from the cottage in the orchard's gold –

From many-acred mansions they are gone,
And from the stithy, and the builder's shed;
By oast and rick and byre there linger on
Old men alone of bowed and hoary head.
While far away the lustful violence fails
Before the men from Britain's peaceful dales.

[Against lines 11-12, 'there linger on / Old men alone'.] This may not have been
literally right, but that is what it felt like in Sussex even at that early date.

[*Poems*, October 1914]

By Chanctonbury

WE shuddered on the blotched and wrinkled down,
So gaunt and chilled with solitary breeze.
Sharp stubborn grass, black-heather trails, wild trees
Knotting their knared wood like a thorny crown –
Huge funnelled dips to chalklands streaked with brown,
White railway smoke-drills dimming by degrees,
Slow ploughs afield, flood waters on the leas,

35

And red roofs of the small, ungainly town:
And blue fog over all, and saddening all –
Thus lay the landscape. Up from the sea there loomed
A stately airship, clear and large awhile:
Then, gliding grandly inland many a mile,
It left our Druid height that black graves plumed,
Vanishing fog-like in the foggy pall.

[*Pastorals*, June 1916]

Uneasy Peace

LATE into the lulling night the pickers toiled,
Stripping still by candle-light the bines uncoiled.
In the valley went and came
The mumbling trains with eyes of flame;
Cold as death is, from the fen
Blue fogs clammed wayfaring men.
    Tolling bells and crouching shades put work away;
    Lurching clowns and kerchered maids closed their long day.

Doors along the hamlet green creaked to and closed.
Lamps were lighted: by the inn some drank, or dozed.
Now keen ears could plainly tell
Bucket splashed in Saunders' well,
Or the passing of the churr,
Or the rainwise elmin's stir.
    Far-off booths by Weston store for folks from town
    Blared and flared an hour more, then dark came down.

Wandering scents of hops at kell, and stragglers' songs,
Dimmed with distance, wove a spell not found in throngs;
Till the people were abed,
Some in tent and some in shed;
Till the twinkling lights went out,
Lost in sleep's gigantic rout;
    Shunting at the station still jangled and banged,
    Still the steel rams by the mill in turmoil clanged.

Soon through oddling eastern yews began to well
Glimmering beauty, golden news from Astrophel:
Dawning of the queen of elves

36

(That loves their dance in toadstool delves) –
Till that moon-enmarvelled sky
Charmed the coy clouds stealing by;
    Till the weir-head shined afar, and dew-dipt meads;
    While men were meditating war with which the world
      still bleeds.

1916

Written in the breastworks at Festubert, May.
[*Poems 1914-30*, December 1930]

The Yellowhammer

WITH rural admixture of shrill and sweet,
Forging his fairy fetter for the ear
Of passing folks, from pollards close the wheat,
The yellowhammer gives the sun a cheer.
    Delighted with his leafy maze
    Like dancing elves he nods and sways,
    And now trills out a chime that's fair,
    And now grates out what he might spare,
While from the totter-grass gazes the humble hare.

1916

Along the canal, Hinges-Essans.
[*Poems 1914-30*, December 1930]

The Festubert Shrine

A SYCAMORE on either side
In whose lovely leafage cried
    Hushingly the little winds –
Thus was Mary's shrine descried.

"Sixteen Hundred and Twenty-Four"
Legended above the door,
    "Pray, sweet gracious Lady, pray
For our souls," – and nothing more.

Builded of rude gray stones and these
Scarred and marred from base to frieze
   With the shrapnel's pounces – ah,
Fair she braved War's gaunt disease:

Fair she pondered on the strange
Embitterments of latter change,
   Looking fair towards Festubert,
Cloven roof and tortured grange.

Work of carving too there was,
(Once had been her reredos),
   In this cool and peaceful cell
That the hoarse guns blared across.

Twisted oaken pillars graced
With oaken amaranths interlaced
   In oaken garlandry, had borne
Her holy niche – and now laid waste.

Mary, pray for us? O pray!
In thy dwelling by this way
   What poor folks have knelt to thee!
We are no less poor than they.

                     May 1916

It *was* a pretty little *chapelle*. Festubert had not many antiquities. But it had the air of a comfortable old village, with plenty of good trees and gardens.

[*Poems 1914-30*, December 1930]

Festubert: The Old German Line

SPARSE mists of moonlight hurt our eyes
With gouged and scourged uncertainties
Of soul and soil in agonies.

One derelict grim skeleton
That drench and dry had battened on
Still seemed to wish us malison;

Still zipped across the gouts of lead
Or cracked like whipcracks overhead;
The gray rags fluttered on the dead.

May 1916

From my first night journey from the cover trench to 'the Islands' over the open.
['Festubert' in the title is crossed out, and inserted before the date at the end of the poem.]

[*Poems 1914-30*, December 1930]

In Festubert[*]

NOW every thing that shadowy thought
    Lets peer with bedlam eyes at me
From alleyways and thoroughfares
    Of incident and memory
Lifts a gaunt head, sullenly stares,
    Shuns me as a child has shunned
A whizzing dragonfly that daps
    Above his mudded pond.

Now bitter frosts, muffling the morn
    In old days, crunch the grass anew;
And where the floods made fields forlorn
    The glinzy ice grows thicker through.
The pollards glower like mummies when
    Thieves break into a pyramid,
Inscrutable as those dead men
    With painted mask and balm-cloth hid;

And all the old delight is cursed
    Redoubling present undelight.
Splinter, crystal, splinter and burst;
    And sear no more with second sight.

1916

I dreamed much, when I was allowed a short sleep at Festubert. My feelings were
still at home, and there were some likenesses in the scene round me, if my old
village had also been under bombardment. As for dreams, indeed some took me
beyond the German lines into queer battles for farms with moats around them &
heavily sandbagged ruins of village streets. [Title crossed out and replaced by 'At
the War'.]

[*The Waggoner*, August 1920]

39

Sheepbells

MOONSWEET the summer evening locks
    The lips of babbling day:
Mournfully, most mournfully
    Light dies away.

There the yew, the solitary,
Vaults a deeper melancholy,
As from distant bells
Chance music wells
From the browsing-bells.

Thus they dingle, thus they chime,
    While the woodlark's dimpling rings
In the dim air climb;
In the dim and dewy loneness
Where the woodlark sings.

        1916

Written at Richebourg I suppose, – but fancifully! [Formerly 'An Evensong'.]
[*Coterie*, No. 3, December 1919
The Waggoner, August 1920]

The New Moon

NEW-SILVER-CRESCENTED the moon forth came
Daring the dark spies of a sullen flaw,
Low-browed: on whom she set her eyes of flame,
And plunged them in swift flight and murmuring awe.
Sweet saffron havens then, and wistful calms
Of infinite dew-crystal palaces,
Were visible through delightful phantom palms,
Blue olive groves, and other dim-plumed trees –
And these but wraiths and cloudy fantasies.
Meantime the reeds, that whispering wind embalms
With whatso spikenard from the white clote came,
Flutter, and home ply hern and pye and daw:

Fearing the firmament to be the Khan
Of grotesque Caliph or blotched Caliban.

1916

Written at Auchy, a mining village where we had a day or two in support. I remember the evening, I walked out and a pond such as I then doted on. The sky was wonderful as I stood there, and the Line was almost silent.

[*Poems 1914-30*, December 1930]

On Turning a Stone[*]

For Alan Porter

TROLLS and pixies unbeknown
Lodged beneath a sunken stone!
Their malevolence makes scream
Children startled in a dream.

O their hundred flickering eyes
Dazzled with day's enterprise –
Skimble-skamble black they run
Scared and seared by shining sun.

1916

[*The Oxford & Cambridge Miscellany*, June 1920
The Waggoner, August 1920]

The Dancer in Thrall

(Thiepval Wood)

I WAS the music in the pines,
　　And in the cascade's cornemute,
Or now a-rustling through the vines
　　I was the West wind's golden lute.

Nor ever in those seqin'd days
　　Was I shut out from dells of Pan,
But in his dewy-tangled maze
　　Deft as a sunbeam laughed and ran.

41

The stars and comets of the night,
   The pell-mell clouds that palled the moon,
The streaming winds, the wind-flowers white,
   Went swaying to my rigadoon.

Who then with curbing hands like chains
   Of carking iron shackled me,
And jarred my songs to motes and grains,
   And lamed my light-heeled revelry?

[*The Blue*, Vol. 44, No. 3, December 1916]

Thiepval Wood*

THE tired air groans as the heavies swing over, the river-hollows boom;
The shell-fountains leap from the swamps, and with wildfire and fume
   The shoulder of the chalkdown convulses.
Then the jabbering echoes stampede in the slatting wood,
Ember-black the gibbet trees like bones or thorns protrude
   From the poisonous smoke – past all impulses.
To them these silvery dews can never again be dear,
Nor the blue javelin-flame of thunderous noons strike fear.

September 1916

At that moment, north of Ancre was comparatively calm. One watched the great
commotion at the south side.

[*Poems 1914-30*, December 1930]

The Condemnation

(Hamel Hill)

"DEATH!" he cried, and, leaden-eyed,
The dull stream through the sallows spied
   A visible fear.
"Death! death!" and, ashen-lipped,
The steely gnomes of water dripped
   Down the weir.

The straining wind, the streaming thicks,
The misty marshes knew black Styx,
   A visible fear.
A troubling moan of tortures wailed
Across the fens; the white house quailed
   By the weir.

Mill, mill, the wheel is still;
The smouldering rust creeps on with a will,
   The weed on the weir.
Green-stained, the rafters fall away,
And bare the cobwebbed laths to the day,
   And none comes near.

G.H.H. ascribes to me ... a far from attractive patrol in the marshes east of Hamel Mill, he asseverates – no slighter term will do – that I announced to him my intention of the patrol and of writing a poem on the Mill, and that I accomplished both. Possibly I told him of the patrol afterwards with poetic licence, at all events, he is sure of it as of the poem, which I actually produced to him. (*Fall In, Ghosts*, p. 252.)

[*Blighty*, Vol. 3, No. 138, 12 February 1919]

"Transport Up" at Ypres*

THE thoroughfares that seem so dead to daylight passers-by
Change character when dark comes down, and traffic starts to ply;
Never a noisier street than the Boulevard Malou becomes
With the cartwheels jolting the dead awake, and the cars like
   rumbling drums.

The crazy houses watch them pass, and stammer with the roar,
The drivers hustle on their mules, more come behind and more;
Briskly the black mules clatter by, to-day was Devil's Mass;
The loathly smell of picric here, and there a touch of gas.

From silhouette to pitchy blur, beneath the bitter stars,
The interminable convoy streams of horses, vans, and cars.
They clamour through the cheerless night, the streets a slattern
   maze,
The sentries at the corners shout them on their different ways.

And so they go, night after night, and chance the shrapnel fire,
The sappers' waggons stowed with frames and concertina wire,
The ration-limbers for the line, the lorries for the guns:
While overhead with fleering light stare down those withered suns.

This pleased George Maycock M.C. our Transport Officer. Jan. 1917.

[*Poems 1914-30*, December 1930]

January Full Moon, Ypres

VANTAGED snow on the gray pilasters
Gleams to the sight so wan and ghostly;
The wolfish shadows in the eerie places
　　Sprawl in the mist-light.

Sharp-fanged searches the frost, and shackles
The sleeping water in broken cellars,
And calm and fierce the witch-moon watches,
　　Curious of evil.

Flares from the horse-shoe of trenches beckon,
Momently soaring and sinking, and often
Peer through the naked fire-swept windows
　　Mocking the fallen.

Quiet, uneasily quiet – the guns hushed,
Scarcely a rifle-shot cracks through the salient,
Only the Cloth Hall sentry's challenge
　　To someone crunching through the frozen snows.

Jan. 1917.

[*Poems 1914-30*, December 1930]

Les Halles d'Ypres

A TANGLE of iron rods and spluttered beams,
　　On brickwork past the skill of a mason to mend:
A wall with a bright blue poster – odd as dreams
　　Is the city's latter end.

A shapeless obelisk looms Saint Martin's spire,
    Now a lean aiming-mark for the German guns;
And the Cloth Hall crouches beside, disfigured with fire,
    The glory of Flanders once.

Only the foursquare tower still bears the trace
    Of beauty that was, and strong embattled age,
And gilded ceremonies and pride of place –
    Before this senseless rage.

And still you may see (below the noon serene,
    The mysterious, changeless vault of sharp blue light),
The pigeons come to the tower, and flaunt and preen,
    And flicker in playful flight.

Jan. 1917.

[*Poems 1914-30*, December 1930]

Clear Weather*

A CLOUDLESS day! with a keener line
    The ruins jut on the glintering blue,
The gas gongs by the billets shine
    Like gold or wine, so trim and new.

Sharp through the wreckage pries the gust,
    And down the roads where wheels have rolled
Whirls the dry snow in powdery dust,
    And starlings muster ruffled with cold.

The gunners profit by the light,
    The guns like surly yard-dogs bark;
And towards Saint Jean in puffs of white
    The anti-aircraft find a mark.

And now the sentries' whistles ply,
    For overhead with whirring drone
An Albatros comes racing by,
    Immensely high, and one of our own

From underneath to meet it mounts,
    And banks and spirals up, and straight
The popping maxims' leaden founts
    Spurt fire, the Boche drops like a weight:

A hundred feet he nose-dives, then
    He rights himself and scuds down sky
Towards the German lines again,
    A great transparent dragon-fly.

Early 1917.

[*Poems 1914-30*, December 1930]

The Cook's Story,
or
Never No More

O 'ave you never 'eard the Tale
    Of Sergeant Bugg's Patrol?
O 'arken, if you 'aven't done,
    Wot come to that poor soul.
Oft times I thinks of 'im, and sighs
With tears fair runnin' from me eyes.

Bugg, everybody knowed ole Bugg,
    A snipin' sergeant 'e;
'E had good taste in Telliscopes,
    Likewise in Rum and Tea;
'E was a clever kind of chap,
I've seen 'im drawin' of a map.

All day within 'is little lair
    'E used to view the Bosch,
'E seen one brushin' of his 'air,
    'E seen another wash,
Quite frequent 'e would see a Cap
(Sof', roun', and Blue) go pass a Gap.

There wasn't nothink Fritz might do
    But Sergint Bugg 'ud spot it;
No periscope as 'e might show
    But Sergint Bugg 'ad got it.
Wy, Fritz 'isself began to shout
'Och, 'och. for Bugg and Sauerkraut.

But as I see you are in 'aste
    Of 'is patrol to 'ear,
I leave aside 'is size in boots
    And 'atred for French beer –
This is the Tale 'e tole to me,
I was a Pal of 'is, you see.

One day, as lookin' from a Post,
    Called Love's Abode for short,
'E saw a Germin orficer
    A-makin' a report –
'E watched 'im passin' thro' the Bays,
Inspecting them Vermonil Sprays.

"Ho, ho!" says Bugg, "is that your game?
    I wants a Medal, too,"
So 'e marks the place upon 'is map
    An' keeps on lookin' through.
The henemy had disappeared,
But Bugg was chortling in 'is Beard.

That night whilst in the ruddy Wess
    Sunk down the blinkin' Sun,
Bugg crep' and crep' upon 'is chess
    Towards the paltry 'Un;
'E 'ad the place marked on 'is map,
'E reached the wire and cut a gap.

On gettin' thro', the Bosch exclaimed,
    " 'Alt! 'oo ARE YOU?" ... "I'm Bugg."
"Come in," says Fritz, "we wants your 'elp,
    'Ere's suthink in a Mug.
We often 'oped as you would come,
We've bin a-savin' you some Rum."

Bugg went ahead as bold as brass,
    The sentry 'elped 'im in;
Another 'anded 'im a glars,
    And fried fish in a tin.
Said Bugg, "I knew you wanted me,
You wants that staff chap pinched, tee hee."

The Fritzes, this wos wot they arsked,
    The staff chap *wos* too keen;
Well, presently 'e comes along
    'An says the Bay 'ain't clean.
"Look 'ere," he says, "this Cartridge Case!
I never seen a dirtier place."

"An' look, that sandbag's not bin brushed;
    'Oo's dropped these crumbs about?"
Bugg stands upon the parapet
    An' whisks the blighter out.
The sentry group discharge their 'ipes
'Igh in the air. An' off Bugg wipes.

'E's got the German by the scruff,
    'E comes towards our lines –
But that young German's much too spruce,
    'E 'isses like an' whines –
'E 'isses like escapin' gas,
The English sentries beat the Brass.

The shrapnel sweeps past poor ole Bugg,
    'E lets the German go;
'E gets a wound in 'is left leg,
    And in 'is big right toe;
'E crawls into our line next day,
The ambulance takes 'im away.

Well, 'e made Blighty, but 'is folk
    Consider 'e is mad,
'Is looks so wild, 'is 'eart so broke –
    The story is most sad;
The bitter tears roll down my mugg
To think of poor old Sergeant Bugg.

Signed 1106 Pte. Alf Maconochie (E.C.B.).

[*The Blue*, Vol. 44, No. 5, March 1917]

Zillebeke Brook

THIS conduit stream that's tangled here and there
With rusted iron and shards of earthenware,
And tawny-stained with ruin trolls across
The tiny village battered into dross –
This muddy water chuckling in its run
Takes wefts of colour from the April sun,
And paints for fancy's eye a glassy burn
Ribanded through a brake of Kentish fern,
From some top spring beside a park's gray pale,
Guarding a shepherded and steepled dale,
Wherefrom the blue deep-coppiced uplands hear
The dim cool noise of waters at a weir.

And much too clear you bring it back to me,
You dreary brook deformed with cruelty,
Here where I halt to catch the day's best mood,
On my way up to Sanctuary Wood.
                                        April 1917

The stream was never recovered, but can be seen still on its way to Zillebeke
Vijver.

[*Poems 1914-30*, December 1930]

Trees on the Calais Road

LIKE mourners filing into church at a funeral,
    These droop their sombre heads and troop to the coast,
The untimely rain makes mystery round them all
    And the wind flies round them like the ghost
    That the body on the blackened trestles lost.

Miserere sobs the weary
Sky, sackclothed, stained, and dreary,
And they bend their heads and sigh
    Miserere, Miserere!

With natural dole and lamentation
They groan for the slaughter and desecration,
But every moment adds to the cry
Of that dead army driving by.

                                        1917

In training about May.

[*Poems 1914-30*, December 1930]

Bleue Maison

NOW to attune my dull soul, if I can,
To the contentment of this countryside
Where man is not for ever killing man
But quiet days like these calm waters glide.
And I will praise the blue flax in the rye,
And pathway bindweed's trumpet-like attire,
Pink rest-harrow and curlock's glistening eye,
And poppies flaring like St. Elmo's fire.

And I will praise the willows silver-gray,
And where I stand the road is rippled over
With airy dreams of blossomed bean and clover,
And shyest birds come elfin-like to play:
And in the rifts of blue above the trees
Pass the full sails of natural Odysseys.

                                        1917

Again not far west of Saint Omer. There *is* a place called something like Bleue
Maison, but I fancy I have got it a bit out of order. What beautiful moments of just
seeing what the world was like, while awaiting what, God knows what.

[*Poems 1914-30*, December 1930]

The Pagoda

FROM the knoll of beeches peeping
On the patterned water sleeping
    Stands the Chinese temple yet,
    Heaped with dead leaves, all alone.

Faded are its amber panels,
Where the channering insect channels,
    And the blood-red dragons fret
    That glared so grimly thereupon.

Mother-pearl and pink shells once
In formal geometricons
    Gemmed the arrassed inner wall,
    But tapestries and frieze are gone.

The small robin reconnoitres,
Unabashed the woodmouse loiters:
    Brown owls hoot at shadow-fall
    And deathwatch ticks and beetles drone.

But I see the shamed pavilion
Bright with yellow and vermilion,
    And, in the sun's hallucination,
    Squired by mandarin Corydon,

Satin-sandalled Chloes glimmering,
Gryphon-urn of Bohea shimmering,
    And the long lost generation
    Seems once more to be my own.

1917

Oddly enough, this was occasioned by my visiting out of curiosity some chateau in ruins along the Menin Road. I suppose a fragment of a summer house was there for a moment or two longer.

[*Poems 1914-30*, December 1930]

Mont de Cassel

HERE on the sunnier scarp of the hill let us rest,
And hoard the hastening hour,
Find a mercy unexpressed
In the chance wild flower
We may find on the pathway side, or the glintering flint,
Or other things so small and unregarded:
Descry far windows fired with the sun, to whom
Nothing is small or mean.
To us, let the war be a leering ghost now shriven,

51

And as though it had never been;
A tragedy mask discarded.
A lamp in a tomb.
What though in the hounded east, now we are gone,
The thunder-throated cannonade boom on?
Too long we have striven,
Too soon we return.
The white stone roads go valleyward from the height,
Like our hopes, to be lost in haze
Where the bonfires burn
With the dross of summer days –
(Our summer hideous, harvesting affright).
Ah, see the silver Spirit dream among his quiet dells,
Hear the slow slumbrous bells,
The voices of a world long by,
Come dim and clear and dim
As the wheat-leys sleep or sigh.
Fall into musings thence, let Psyche stray
Where she lists,
Among small things of little account,
Or through the coloured mists; –
Myriad the roads to the visionary mount,
And the white forehead of the Mystery.
  But alas, she falls in a swoon,
  Pale-lipped like a withering moon;
So terrible is the insistency
Of the east where like a fiend automaton
The thunder-throated cannonade booms on.

September 1917

When I was at Zuytpeene on a course of instruction. It was a dull time, but Cassell Hill still rose above it, and I went up hopefully to enjoy civilization there.

[*The Waggoner*, August 1920]

The Sighing Time

THE sighing time, the sighing time! ...
  The old house mourns and shudders so;
  And the bleak garrets' crevices
  Like whirring distaffs utter dread;
  Streams of shadow people go

By hollow stairs and passages
In black cloths herding out their dead.
Along the creaking corridors
They troop with sighs, grayhead and young,
They droop their heads in bitter tears.
The panels yawn like charnel doors
Where the dark windows ivy-clung
Are gloating spiders' belvederes.
Without, like old Laocoön,
The yewtree claws the serpent gusts,
The wicket swings with peacock screams.
Time in the courtyard leans upon
His pausing scythe, in dim mistrusts
And sad recalls of summer dreams.
The garden, cynically sown
With leaves in death unlovely, bows
Its tragic plume of pipy stalks:
Poison-spores have overgrown
In crazy-coloured death-carouse
The parterres and the lovers' walks.
The anguished sun is swiftly set,
And Hesper's primrose coronal
Is sullied with distortions pale.
The grange bell in its minaret
With dreary three-times-dreary call
    Dingles in the gale.
The sighing time, the sighing time.

1917

A recollection of Congelow. Autumn?

[*The Waggoner*, August 1920]

Clare's Ghost

PITCH-DARK night shuts in, and the rising gale
   Is full of the presage of rain,
   And there comes a withered wail
   From the wainscot and jarring pane,
   And a long funeral surge
   Like a wood-god's dirge,
Like the wash of the shoreward tides, from the firs on the crest.

The shaking hedges blacken, the last gold flag
   Lowers from the West;
The Advent bell moans wild like a witch hag
   In the storm's unrest,
And the lychgate lantern's candle weaves a shroud,
   And the unlatched gate shrieks loud.

Up fly the smithy sparks, but are baffled from soaring
   By the pelting scurry, and ever
As puff the bellows, a multitude more outpouring
   Die foiled in the endeavour.

And a stranger stands with me here in the glow
Chinked through the door, and marks
   The sparks
Perish in whirlpool wind, and if I go
To the delta of cypress, where the glebe gate cries,
I see him there, with his streaming hair
   And his eyes
Piercing beyond our human firmament,
Lit with a burning deathless discontent.

1917

Written in war surroundings, from Framfield memories. [Formerly 'Phantasies'.]

[*The Blue*, Vol. 45, No. 1, October 1917
The Waggoner, August 1920]

The Unchangeable[*]

THOUGH I within these two last years of grace
Have seen bright Ancre scourged to brackish mire,
And meagre Belgian becks by dale and chace
Stamped into sloughs of death with battering fire –
Spite of all this, I sing you high and low,
My old loves, Waters, be you shoal or deep,
Waters whose lazy and continual flow
Learns at the drizzling weir the tongue of sleep.
And Sussex cries from primrose lags and brakes,
"Why do you leave my woods untrod so long?
Still float the bronze carp on my lilied lakes,
Still the wood-fairies round my spring wells throng;

And chancing lights on willowy waterbreaks
Dance to the bubbling brooks of elfin song."

1917

Looking our from Larch Wood Tunnels on the railway cutting.

[*Coterie*, No. 3, December 1919
The Waggoner, August 1920]

The Weathercock

THE turret's leaden carapace
  Is shining coldly in the moon,
  And the winds are in a swoon.
And sad and tarnished, into space,
Pinnacled in the highest place,
  The little golden boy forlorn
  Blows on his hunting-horn.

Call as you may, call as you may,
  You little airy forester,
  The winds will yet demur.
And the harried ghosts may saunter and stray
Untroubled with the swelling bay
  Of the straining hounds of the wind-god, till
  The red sun climbs the smoking hill.

The air's intense with iron frost;
  And you are fettered, golden boy,
  Nor spin in mad-heart joy.
But even now the die is tossed
That bids the winter yield his power,
And soon again upon your tower,
You'll trumpet through the raining night
  The wind's delight,
  The ghost's affright,
The roistering hunter-gale's delight.

Flanders, 1917

These verses were written by way of recreation in the Ypres Salient towards the end of 1917. At that time a habit of reading French verse characterized the author and explains these stanzas! If any apology be required as well, let it be recalled that 'there was a war on' – and such relics have their own value to those who remember it.

[Title page to *The Weathercock – La Girouette*, Paris, Ulysses Bookshop, 1931]

THE SHEPHERD RETURNS

A Country God*

WHEN groping farms are lanterned up
    And stolchy ploughlands hid in grief,
And glimmering byroads catch the drop
    That weeps from sprawling twig and leaf,
And heavy-hearted spins the wind
    Among the tattered flags of Mirth, –
Then who but I flit to and fro,
With shuddering speech, with mope and mow,
    And glass the eyes of Earth?

Then haunting by some moanish brook
    Where lank and snaky brambles swim,
Or where the hill pines swartly look
    I whirry through the dark and hymn,
A dull-voiced dirge and threnody,
    An echo of the world's sad drone
That now appals the friendly stars –
O wail for blind brave youth whose wars
    Turn happiness to stone.

How rang the cavern-shades of old
    To my melodious pipes, and then
My bright-haired bergamask patrolled
    Each lawn and plot for laughter's din:
Never a sower flung broad cast,
    No hedger brished nor scythesman swung,
Nor maiden trod the purpling press
But I was by to guard and bless
    And for their solace sung.

But now the sower's hand is writhed
In livid death, the bright rhythm stolen,
The gold grain flattened and unscythed,
The boars in the vineyard gnarled and sullen
Havocking the grapes; and the pouncing wind
Spins the spattered leaves of the glen
In a mockery dance, death's hue-and-cry;
With all my murmurous pipes flung by
And summer not to come again.

1918

On leaving France, Feb. 25th, 1918.

[*The Owl*, No. 2, 25 October 1919
The Waggoner, August 1920]

Wild Cherry Tree

HERE be rural graces, sylvan places,
Bright-hearted brooks that chanting fall,
Leys and fallows, reedy rustling shallows,
Colours and musics rustical.

O the silvery cherry, the visionary,
Templed in dewy dim green pleasance
Where moths flutter bloom-like – who shall utter
The shining wonder of her presence?

Nor shall midnight veil her, hushed moon fail her,
Nor lack true lover then shall she;
Breathed from sleeping orchards afar shall come creeping
A long long sigh to the darling tree.

1918

In camp in Anglia I think.

[*Poems 1914-30*, December 1930]

A Vignette

BRONZE noonlight domes the dim blue gloom
Where many-antlered oaks immure
A hush, a cool – the "cynosure
Of neighbouring eyes," that tired with bloom
And blaze of poppied yellowing swath,
And jewelled meadows' pomp and state,
Delight to spy the glimmering gate
Far down the oakwood's bridle-path.

A fancy.
[*Poems 1914-30*, December 1930]

Malefactors

NAILED to these green laths long ago,
You cramp and shrivel into dross,
Blotched with mildews, gnawed with moss,
And now the eye can scarcely know
The snake among you from the kite,
    So sharp does Death's fang bite.

I guess your stories; you were shot
Hovering above the miller's chicks;
And you, coiled on his threshold bricks –
Hissing you died; and you, sir Stoat,
Dazzled with stableman's lantern stood
    And tasted crabtree wood.

Here then you leered-at luckless churls,
Clutched to your clumsy gibbet, shrink
To shapeless orts; hard by the brink
Of this black scowling pond that swirls
To turn the wheel beneath the mill,
    The wheel so long since still.

There's your revenge, the wheel at tether,
The miller gone, the white planks rotten,
The very name of the mill forgotten,
Dimness and silence met together.
Felons of fur and feather, can
   There lurk some crime in man,

In man your executioner,
Whom here Fate's cudgel battered down?
Did he too filch from squire and clown?
The damp gust makes the ivy whir
Like passing death; the sluices well,
   Dreary as a passing-bell.

1919

[*The Waggoner*, August 1920]

The Veteran

For G.H. Harrison

HE stumbles silver-haired among his bees,
Now with the warm sun mantling him; he plods
Taking his honey under the pippin-trees,
Where every sprig with rich red harvest nods.
   He marks the skies' intents,
And like a child, his joy still springing new,
In this fantastic garden the year through
He steeps himself in nature's opulence.

Mellow between the leafy maze smiles down
September's sun, swelling his multitude
Of gold and red and green and russet-brown
Lavished in plenty's lusty-handed mood
   For this old man who goes
Reckoning ripeness, shoring the lolling sprays,
And fruits which early gusts made castaways –
From the deep grasses thriftily rescuing those.

Babble he will, lingeringly, lovingly,
Of all the glories of this fruitful place,
Counting the virtues of each several tree,
Her years, her yield, her hardihood or grace;
   While through this triumph-song,
As through their shielding leaves, the year's fruits burn
In bright eye-cozening colour, turn by turn,
From cool black cherries till gold quinces throng

Blossoming the blue mists with their queenly scent.
Who hearing him can think what dragging years
Of drouthy raids and frontier-fights he spent,
With drum and fife to drown his clamouring fears?
   Here where the grapes turn red
On the red walls, and honey in the hives
Is like drift snow, contentment only thrives,
And the long misery of the Line is dead.

Resting in his old oaken-raftered room,
He sits and watches the departing light
Crimsoning like his apple-trees in bloom,
With dreaming gratitude and calm delight.
   And fast the peering sun
Has lit the blue delft ranged along the wall,
The painted clock and Squirrel's Funeral,
And through the cobwebs traced his rusty gun.

And then the dusk, and sleep, and while he sleeps,
Apple-scent floods and honey's fragrance there,
And old-time wines, whose secret he still keeps,
Are beautiful upon the marvelling air.
   And if sleep seem unsound,
And set old bugles pealing through the dark,
Waked on the instant, he but wakes to hark
His bellman cockerel crying the first round.

1919

[*The Nation*, 1 November 1919
The Waggoner, August 1920]

The Pike*

FROM shadows of rich oaks outpeer
The moss-green bastions of the weir,
Where the quick dipper forages
In elver-peopled crevices.
And a small runlet trickling down the sluice
Gossamer music tires not to unloose.

Else round the broad pool's hush
   Nothing stirs.
Unless sometime a straggling heifer crush
Through the thronged spinney whence the pheasant whirs;
   Or martins in a flash
Come with wild mirth to dip their magical wings,
While in the shallow some doomed bulrush swings
   At whose hid root the diver vole's teeth gnash.

And nigh this toppling reed, still as the dead
   The great pike lies, the murderous patriarch,
   Watching the waterpit shelving and dark
Where through the plash his lithe bright vassals thread.

   The rose-finned roach and bluish bream
   And staring ruffe steal up the stream
   Hard by their glutted tyrant, now
   Still as a sunken bough.
   He on the sandbank lies,
     Sunning himself long hours
   With stony gorgon eyes:
     Westward the hot sun lowers.

Sudden the gray pike changes, and quivering poises for
    slaughter;
  Intense terror wakens around him, the shoals scud awry, but
    there chances
  A chub unsuspecting; the prowling fins quicken, in fury he
    lances;
And the miller that opens the hatch stands amazed at the whirl
    in the water.

1919

Generalized, – Cheveney, Heaver's Mill & c.

[*Coterie*, No. 3, December 1919
The Waggoner, August 1920 (revised)]

The Estrangement

DIM through cloud vails the moonlight trembles down
A cold grey vapour on the huddling town;
And far from cut-throat's corner the eye sees
Unsilvered hogs'-backs, pallid stubble-leas;
Barn-ridges gaunt and gleamless: blue like ghosts
The knoll mill and the odd cowls of the oasts,
And lonely homes pondering with joys and fears
The dusty travail of three hundred years.

In the ashen twilight momently afield,
Like thistle-wool wafting across the weald,
Flickers a sighing spirit; as he passes,
The lispering aspens and the scarfed brook grasses
With wakened melancholy writhe the air.

In the false moonlight wails my old despair,
And I am but a pipe for its wild moan;
Crying through the misty bypaths; slumber-banned;
Impelled and voiced, to piercing coronach blown:

A hounded kern in this grim No Man's Land,
I am spurned between the secret countersigns
Of every little grain of rustling sand
In these parched lanes where the grey wind maligns;
Oaks, once my friends, with ugly murmurings
Madden me, and ivy whirs like condor wings:
The very bat that stoops and whips askance
Shrills malice at the soul grown strange in France.

1919

Formerly 'Estrangement'.

[*Voices*, Vol. 3, No. 1, February 1920
The Waggoner, August 1920 (revised)]

Perch-Fishing

for G.W. Palmer

ON the far hill the cloud of thunder grew
And sunlight blurred below: but sultry blue
Burned yet on the valley water where it hoards
Behind the miller's elmen floodgate boards,
And there the wasps, that lodge them ill-concealed
In the vole's empty house, still drove afield
To plunder touchwood from old crippled trees
And build their young ones their hutched nurseries;
Still creaked the grasshoppers' rasping unison
Nor had the whisper through the tansies run
Nor weather-wisest bird gone home.
                                    How then
Should wry eels in the pebbled shallows ken
Lightning coming? troubled up they stole
To the deep-shadowed sullen water-hole,
Among whose warty snags the quaint perch lair.

As cunning stole the boy to angle there,
Muffling least tread, with no noise balancing through
The hangdog alder-boughs his bright bamboo.
Down plumbed the shuttled ledger, and the quill
On the quicksilver water lay dead still.

A sharp snatch, swirling to-fro of the line,
He's lost, he's won, with splash and scuffling shine
Past the low-lapping brandy-flowers drawn in,
The ogling hunchback perch with needled fin.
And there beside him one as large as he,
Following his hooked mate, careless who shall see
Or what befall him, close and closer yet –
The startled boy might take him in his net
That folds the other.
                        Slow, while on the clay
The other flounces, slow he sinks away.

What agony usurps that watery brain
For comradeship of twenty summers slain,
For such delights below the flashing weir

64

And up the sluice-cut, playing buccaneer
Among the minnows; lolling in hot sun
When bathing vagabonds had drest and done;
Rootling in salty flannel-weed for meal
And river shrimps, when hushed the trundling wheel;
Snapping the dapping moth, and with new wonder
Prowling through old drowned barges falling asunder.
And O a thousand things the whole year through
They did together, never more to do.

1919

The 2 large perch were taken by me at Langridge's Pond, Yalding, & surprised Mr Langridge, who I think is still there – but the pond is nothing today.

[*A Queen's College Miscellany*, June 1920
The Waggoner, August 1920]

Spring Night

THROUGH the smothered air the wicker finds
A muttering voice, 'crick' cries the embered ash,
Sharp rains knap at the panes beyond the blinds,
The flues and eaves moan, the jarred windows clash;
And like a sea breaking its barriers, flooding
New green abysses with untold uproar,
The cataract nightwind whelms the time of budding,
Swooping in sightless fury off the moor
Into our valley. Not a star shines. Who
Would guess the martin and the cuckoo come,
The pear in bloom, the bloom gone from the plum,
The cowslips countless as a morning dew?
So mad it blows, so truceless and so grim,
As if day's host of flowers were a moment's whim.

Boar's Hill surely 1920 or 21.

[*Voices*, Vol. 4, No. 4, October 1920
The Shepherd, April 1922]

Blindfold

FROM the mirror-hall of sleep
    Morning's phaeton beckons me,
Like an exile out I creep
    Into a new mystery,
Hurrying from the threshold stone
As though forced to walk alone.

Silver webs shake wet and cold,
    Like a drugget drops the mist,
Snake-skins lie below the fold,
    Lean leaves touched with ague twist,
While the puffing wind-god breathes
Dew-fog into drifting wreathes.

Shrill and surly sound the cocks,
    Their cry ends with mist beyond,
Late-departing yelps the fox,
    Strangely sounds the madpit pond,
Where among the blackening sedge
Cranking water-wildfowl dredge.

All the country seems alone,
    Nothing has a comrade now,
With a solitary moan
    The very mill-stream skulks a-low,
Running in obscurity
To a sightless destiny.

[*To-day*, Vol. 7, No. 41, July 1920
To Nature, June 1923 (revised)]

Death of Childhood Beliefs

THERE the puddled lonely lane,
   Lost among the red swamp sallows,
Gleams through drifts of summer rain
   Down to ford the sandy shallows,
Where the dewberry brambles crane.

And the stream in cloven clay
   Round the bridging sheep-gate stutters,
Wind-spun leaves burn silver-grey,
   Far and wide the blue moth flutters
Over swathes of warm new hay.

Scrambling boys with mad to-do
   Paddle in the sedges' hem,
Ever finding joy anew;
   Clocks toll time out – not for them,
With what years to frolic through!

How shall I return and how
   Look once more on those old places!
For Time's cloud is on me now
   That each day, each hour effaces
Visions once on every bough.

Stones could talk together then,
   Jewels lay for hoes to find,
Each oak hid King Charles agen,
   Ay, nations in his powdered rind;
Sorcery lived with homeless men.

Spider Dick, with cat's green eyes
   That could pierce stone walls, has flitted –
By some hedge he shakes and cries,
   A lost man, half-starved, half-witted,
Whom the very stoats despise.

Trees on hill-tops then were Palms,
   Closing pilgrims' arbours in;
David walked there singing Psalms;

67

Out of the clouds white seraphin
Leaned to watch us fill our bin.

Where's the woodman now to tell
    Will o' the Wisp's odd fiery anger?
Where's the ghost to toll the bell
    Startling midnight with its clangour
Till the wind seemed but a knell?

Drummers jumping from the tombs
    Banged and thumped all through the town,
Past shut shops and silent rooms
    While the flaming spires fell down;–
Now but dreary thunder booms.

Smuggler trapped in headlong spate,
    Smuggler's mare with choking whinney,
Well I knew your fame, your fate;
    By the ford and shaking spinney
Where you perished I would wait,

Half in glory, half in fear,
    While the fierce flood, trough and crest,
Whirled away the shepherd's gear,
    And sunset wildfire coursed the west,
Crying Armageddon near.

Kent is the scene here.

[*The Athenaeum*, 8 October 1920
The Shepherd, April 1922]

The Forest

AMONG the golden groves when June walketh there
I go to find old loves in the haunted air,
And with the humble bee down the ancient rides
I pause whene'er I see where my honey hides.

But scarcely now I heed the small welcome moss
Or time's secrets read or pore on pit and fosse,
Or kindle at blooms I knew not before,
Though twayblade haunt the glooms and strange hellebore.

68

THE SHEPHERD RETURNS

The pheasant crows anear, I lift not my head;
Wildcats race in fear – as well flee the dead!
Oaks breathe and pines sigh, and all for praise,
And yet my soul divines little that each says:

But the whole wood moves again and again
Memory of old loves, perfect joy of pain;
Without words I've found the hid world at last
In the woods deep drowned, after so long past:

Not my first delight, the sweet Kentish girl,
Once ever in my sight, but gone, gone in the whirl
Of time's broken stream, till I cannot guess
Her smile or primrose gleam of new loveliness:

Not my childhood's bliss, in greenwoods to go
Where great snakes might hiss, so high reeds did grow,
And from early day till eve trembling crept,
Pioneers to stray where the black ponds slept:

But the rich hours chance gave, where dry-lipped with war
I left him to rave on his ridges not far,
And lay in a green shade of Aveluy Wood
And with those hours allayed the fever in the blood;

Not a leaf regarding, but one with the wood's soul,
All my thoughts discarding – refreshed thence and whole
I went to live or die, and five years are flown,
But not till now was I with the woods again alone.

[*Nation & Athenaeum*, 25 June 1921
The Shepherd, April 1922]

IMPACTS OF WAR

11th R.S.R.

HOW bright a dove's wing shows against the sky
When thunder's blackening up in monstrous cloud;
How silver clear against war's hue and cry
Each syllable of peace the gods allowed!
Even common things in anguish have grown rare
As legends of a richer life gone by,
Like flowers that in their time were no one's care,
But blooming late are loved and grudged to die.

What mercy is it I should live and move,
If haunted ever by war's agony?
Nature is love and will remember love,
And kindly uses those whom fear set free.
Let me not even think of you as dead,
O never dead! you live, your old songs yet
Pass me each day, your faith still routs my dread,
Your past and future are my parapet.

You looked before and after! these calm shires,
The doting sun, the orchards all aflame,
These joyful flocking swallows round the spires,
Bonfires and turreted stacks – well may you claim,
Still seeing these sweet familiar bygones, all!
Still dwells in you their has-been, their to-be,
And walking in their light you fear no fall.
This is your holding: mine, across the sea,

Where much I find to trace old friendship by:
"Here one bade us farewell," "Here supped we then,"
"Wit never sweeter fell than that July" –
Even sometimes comes the praise of better men.
The land lies like a jewel in the mind,
And featured sharp shall lie when other fades,

And through its veins the eternal memories wind
As that lost column down its colonnades.

Flat parcelled fields the scanty paths scored through,
Woods where no guns thrust their lean muzzles out,
Small smoky inns, we laughed at war's ado!
And clutching death, to hear, fell into doubt.
Christ at each crossroad hung, rich belfries tolling,
Old folks a-digging, weathercocks turned torches,
Half-hearted railways, flimsy millsails rolling –
Not one, but by the host for ever marches.

How *happy* the Battalion was in ordinary country places!

[*The Shepherd*, April 1922]

Behind the Line

TREASURE not so the forlorn days
When dun clouds flooded the naked plains
   With foul remorseless rains;
   Tread not those memory ways
Where by the dripping alien farms,
Starved orchards with their shrivelled arms,
The bitter mouldering wind would whine
At the brisk mules clattering towards the Line.

Remember not with so sharp skill
Each chasm in the clouds that strange with fire
   Lit pyramid-fosse and spire
   Miles on miles from our hill;
In the magic glass, aye, then their lure
Like heaven's houses gleaming pure
Might soothe the long-imprisoned sight
And put the double storm to flight.

Enact not you so like a wheel
The round of evenings in sandbagged rooms
   Where candles flicked the glooms;
   The jests old time could steal
From ugly destiny, on whose brink
The poor fools grappled fear with drink,
And snubbed the hungry raving guns
With endless tunes on gramophones.

About you spreads the world anew,
The old fields all for your sense rejoice,
   Music has found her ancient voice,
   From the hills there's heaven on earth to view.
And kindly Mirth will raise his glass
With you to bid dull Care go pass –
And still you wander muttering on
Over the shades of shadows gone.

Some of us were driven back by the world of peace and its puzzles to the company
of the years of terror.

[*The Shepherd*, April 1922]

The Avenue

UP the long colonnade I press, and strive
By love to thank God that I go alive:
And the night dark as palls of cloud can prove
Bids me seek beauty, while wetshod I move,
In the scarce-glimmering boles and flying boughs
That run up black and naked to Heaven's brows
And are as still as life could ever be.
Thus think I trudging on to know each tree,
This leaning out of line; that with great rings,
Ay, ruffs of gnarled grain, whence the forked top springs;
That with its crow's nest; one whose boughs stoop down
Like roots into the sward below; one's crown
Struck by the lightning, whence it stands alone
Stark staring mad but dead, its own tombstone.

And still trees, trees; long lies the journey through,
Till the thought runs like rebel dogs askew,
And soon one tree is like the rest a tree:
If stunt or sturdy, all are one to me.
While men ahead, behind and left and right,
Tramp over the greasy cobbles through midnight,
Between great monolith trees, and often throw
Their strapped packs up to ease them, as they go
Half in a sleep, brain-cramped, dead though they live;
And those who speak find but few words to give.

Drenchingly dripped the trees, the blown sleet came,
These trees were jagged with worse than lightning's flame,
These fields were gouged with worse than ploughs, a moan
Worse than the wind's with every wind went on.
The rattling limbers hurrying past would jar
The jangled nerves, and candles' chancing gleam
From sweating cellars looked sweet peace as far
As any star and wilder than a dream
To him who soon would be beyond the wire
Listening his wits to ague in the mire,
And waiting till the drumfire hours began,
In the fool's triumph of the soul of man:
Beneath those lights whose fountain-play would shine
On quiet hamlets miles behind the line,
That in our respite we had watched ascend,
And poise their drooped heads scouring end to end
The grey front lines; and plucking at death's sleeve
They showed him in the nick new skulls to cleave,
Yet never once lit up our destiny,
But moped and mowed in dizzy secrecy.
Now on the sky I see the dull lights burn
Of that small village whither I return.
The trees hide backward in the mists, the men
Are lying in their thankless graves agen,
And I a stranger in my home pass by
To seek and serve the beauty that must die.

Near Newmarket.

[*London Mercury*, Vol. 3, No. 16, February 1921
The Shepherd, April 1922]

Reunion in War

THE windmill in his smock of white
    Stared from his little crest,
Like a slow smoke was the moonlight
    As I went like one possessed

Where the glebe path makes shortest way;
    The stammering wicket swung.

I passed amid the crosses grey
    Where opiate yew-boughs hung.

The bleached grass shuddered into sighs,
    The dogs that knew this moon
Far up were harrying sheep, the cries
    Of hunting owls went on.

And I among the dead made haste
    And over flat vault stones
Set in the path unheeding paced
    Nor thought of those chill bones.

Thus to my sweetheart's cottage I,
    Who long had been away,
Turned as the traveller turns adry
    To brooks to moist his clay.

Her cottage stood like a dream, so clear
    And yet so dark; and now
I thought to find my more than dear
    And if she'd kept her vow.

Old house-dog from his barrel came
    Without a voice, and knew
And licked my hand; all seemed the same
    To the moonlight and the dew.

By the white damson then I took
    The tallest osier wand
And thrice upon her casement strook,
    And she, so fair, so fond,

Looked out, and saw in wild delight,
    And tiptoed down to me,
And cried in silent joy that night
    Beside the bullace tree.

O cruel time to take away,
    Or worse to bring agen;
Why slept not I in Flanders clay
    With all the murdered men?

For I had changed, or she had changed,
    Though true loves both had been,

Even while we kissed we stood estranged
     With the ghosts of war between.

We had not met but a moment ere
     War baffled joy, and cried,
"Love's but a madness, a burnt flare;
     The shell's a madman's bride."

The cottage stood, poor stone and wood,
     Poorer than stone stood I;
Then from her kind arms moved in a mood
     As grey as the cereclothed sky.

The roosts were stirred, each little bird
     Called fearfully out for day;
The church clock with his dead voice whirred
     As if he bade me stay

To trace with foolish fingers all
     The letters on the stones
Where thick beneath the twitch roots crawl
     In dead men's envied bones.

Imagined, but based on some mood during leave.

[*The Nation*, 20 November 1920
The Shepherd, April 1922]

A Farm near Zillebeke

BLACK clouds hide the moon, the amazement is gone;
The morning will come in weeping and rain;
The Line is all hushed – on a sudden anon
The fool bullets clack and guns mouth again.
I stood in the yard of a house that must die,
And still the black hame was stacked by the door,
And harness still hung there, and the dray waited by.

Black clouds hid the moon, tears blinded me more.

Early 1917, farm near 'Vince Street', it had not long to wait.

[*The Shepherd*, April 1922]

1916 seen from 1921

TIRED with dull grief, grown old before my day,
I sit in solitude and only hear
Long silent laughters, murmurings of dismay,
The lost intensities of hope and fear;
In those old marshes yet the rifles lie,
On the thin breastwork flutter the grey rags,
The very books I read are there – and I
Dead as the men I loved, wait while life drags

Its wounded length from those sad streets of war
Into green places here, that were my own;
But now what once was mine is mine no more,
I seek such neighbours here and I find none.
With such strong gentleness and tireless will
Those ruined houses seared themselves in me,
Passionate I look for their dumb story still,
And the charred stub outspeaks the living tree.

I rise up at the singing of a bird
And scarcely knowing slink along the lane,
I dare not give a soul a look or word
Where all have homes and none's at home in vain:
Deep red the rose burned in the grim redoubt,
The self-sown wheat around was like a flood,
In the hot path the lizard lolled time out,
The saints in broken shrines were bright as blood.

Sweet Mary's shrine between the sycamores!
There we would go, my friend of friends and I,
And snatch long moments from the grudging wars,
Whose dark made light intense to see them by.
Shrewd bit the morning fog, the whining shots
Spun from the wrangling wire; then in warm swoon
The sun hushed all but the cool orchard plots,
We crept in the tall grass and slept till noon.

Formerly 'Festubert, 1916'.

[*The New Keepsake for the Year 1921*, December 1920
The Shepherd, April 1922]

The Troubled Spirit

SAID God, Go, spirit, thou hast served me well
In these our palaces, and choose out one star
Of all the universe beneath us lies,
And see what other beauty I have made.
So spoke the Almighty, in whose eyes there burned
A dimmer light, and whose bowed head revealed
Some weariness: while Time smiled to himself.

Now takes the spirit thought, whether to search
The rosy fires of suns innumerable
That seem not to have rest even for a spirit,
Or to some tinier satellite to fly
And kindlier radiance beckoning.
                                    Thus comes he
To earth, and sees the restless water curve
Round lands wherefrom a rumour smokes, scarce loud
As the voices of the waters, and there seems
In these lands but a quiet interchange
Of music, jarred, yet nigh to full concent.
So comes the spirit.
                        And now, passing among
The moving multitude, he sees how most
Are strong and lusty in their generation,
And though their countenance to their fellows yield
Small comfort, yet the most seem in themselves
To find all that this world might ever give.
The ringing cities shine in the morning light
And in the evening glitter unafraid,
The beasts are droved to furnish their proud tables.
The deeps yield up their mystery for their need.

Over the green fields, over the silver waters
Goes the good spirit, and earth's willing plenty
Warms him to rapture, while the zeal and power
Of busy man, thinks he, is the bright flower
Of all besides; nay even the songs of heaven
Scarce seem so brave, and though death takes his toll,
The strong still flourish, and the grief's soon past.

But now the poursuivant, making swift way,
Happy as swallows in the blue calm air,
While the rich harvest glows and the hives rejoice,
Espies a wilderness where little's green,
And the land clawed as by great dragon's pounces
Yet dumb, dun, mournful lieth by itself,
With wounds ten thousand times ten thousand writhed.

Over this golgotha poising like a kestrel
He stares, he wonders – here the very quiet
Is a vast hubbub, here the sun's uprising
Is the annihilation of night's mercy,
The fallen jaw grins, the eyes are glazed with foulness.
O Spirit, fly thy swiftest!
                              Pondering deep
He leaves the brown waste far away, he comes
To a white village peeping through its elms.
There he stoops down and in a coppice rests.

The twilight now bids timid hares come forth
And play like children in the woodside corn,
Hot youth flings by, and age as bold though slow,
But one there trembling comes where rests the spirit,
And stands half silent, as for very shame
To himself muttering. Yet the spirit looks
And sees his eyes as eyes set earnestly
On some one listening and of one mind with him.

Where the soul's uttered, though the words be halt,
They are a language understood in heaven,
And thus the spirit, now first listening close,
Hears not unwitting.
                         "Like a ghost am I,
Having no part in common day or joy,
Young, and yet older than the oldest men.
There's none to understand though some may love.
Nay, those might understand would shun to open
Their heart, but bind old memories as with chains.

Has summer come? and has she passed her noon?
How once I told myself of summer coming
When I'd amaze myself with every minute
From the first thrill of day till midnight hawks
Laughed bedlam down the hedge – if I should live
To see those magic summers. And I live;

But now the moss upon the churchyard stone
Has felt the radiance with a joy not mine,
And summer seems a rumour in the past.

So high flamed life when death was gesturing by,
So faint burns now. A day of that gone age
Was more than all the days that now shall come.
Then friendship was, that mightier grew than love.
Why are you fallen, friend after friend? for these
Lie now lapt in their silence and the clay
Whose stubborn hatred they so often fought,
And these are scattered listless and estranged.
All climbed the summits of the immense, all learned
The secrets of the tempest and the dawn,
In Zara desert now all bleach or crawl.

But come you, friends, let necromantic thought
Be our reunion; find we our old selves
And our old haunts, half-stricken towns that dare
Keep mirth alive, old cellars and rare sleep,
Lines where glad poppies burn or pollards stalk,
And terror broods not greater than we can bear,
Sleep's double sweet, wit twice as precious there.
And there joy triumphs, from such danger snatcht,
And there we'll sit and make our sad selves merry,
Nor reckon up to-morrow and its fate;
Enjoy the franchise of wild-running nature,
Nor prophesy to-morrow's maniac battle.
Fine merry franions ———"
                            Tears no words can tell
Fall now; the spirit goes abroad attuned
To this wild mood, and hears it from all sides,
And musing with a dimness on his brow
The wreck of earth, the soul's worse solitude,
Returns to heaven, is stationed by the throne,
And now first sees how the bowed head reveals
Some weariness, while Time smiles to himself.

[*The Shepherd*, April 1922]

The Late Stand-to

I THOUGHT of cottages nigh brooks
    Whose aspens loved to shine and swirl,
Of chubby babies' wondering looks
    Above the doorboards, and the girl
Who blossomed like the morning sky,
    With clear light like a lily made;
She dipt her bucket and went by,
    Where bright the unwithering water played.

No water ever ran so blithe
    As that same mill-tail stream, I'd say,
And life as laughing danced as lithe
    And twinkled on as many a day.
The wonder seemed that summer waned,
    So full it filled the giant sphere,
But skulls chill on where warm blood reigned
    And even such summers must grow sere.

I heard the bell brag on the west
    And whisper on the eastern wind,
And hated how it found the nest
    That Time was never meant to find:
Through many an afternoon blue-hung
    Like sultry smoke with drowsy heat
There came the bell-cote's scheming tongue
    Till gipsy-boys that slouched down street

With roach on withy rods impaled
    Had flown, and swallows met to fly,
And yellow light and leaves prevailed
    And trouble roved the evening sky.
But spite of ghosts who shook their hair
    In clouds and stalked through darker plains,
Still to the wood bridge I'd repair
    Ere autumn palsied into rains.

The fish turned over in the shoal,
    A flash of summer! then came she,
Who when green leaves were lapping cool
    So like a lily dazzled me;

Her basketful of mushrooms got,
    She passed, she called me by my name,
And now whole myriads are forgot
    But kindly Nell will seem the same

Down to my death! Long tarry, Sun,
    That shone upon us two that day,
And autumn's honey breath live on
    The last sighed air that leaves me clay! –
Clay! clay! the packing bullets mocked
    And split the breastwork by my head,
And into aching senses shocked
    I gave Stand-To! the east was red.

[*London Mercury*, Vol. 5, No. 27, January 1922
The Shepherd, April 1922]

War Autobiography

Written in illness

HEAVEN is clouded, mists of rain
Stream with idle motion by;
Like a tide the trees' refrain
Wearies me where pale I lie,
Thinking of sunny times that were
Even in shattered Festubert;
Stubborn joys that blossomed on
When the small golden god was gone

Who tiptoe on his spire surveyed
Yser north from Ypres creeping,
And, how many a sunset! made
A longed-for glory amid the weeping.
In how many a valley of death
Some trifling thing has given me breath,
And when the bat-like wings brushed by
What steady stars smiled in the sky!

War might make his worst grimace,
And still my mind in armour good
Turned aside in every place
And saw bright day through the black wood:

There the lyddite vapoured foul,
But there I got myself a rose;
By the shrapnelled lock I'd prowl
To see below the proud pike doze.

Like the first light ever streamed
New and lively past all telling,
When I dreamed of joy I dreamed,
The more opprest the more rebelling;
Trees ne'er shone so lusty green
As those in Hamel valley, eyes
Did never such right friendship mean
As his who loved my enterprise.

Thus the child was born again
In the youth, the toga's care
Flung aside – desired, found vain,
And sharp as ichor grew the air:
But the hours passed and evermore
Harsher screamed the condor war,
The last green tree was scourged to nothing,
The stream's decay left senses loathing,

The eyes that had been strength so long
Gone, or blind, or lapt in clay,
And war grown twenty times as strong
As when I held him first at bay;
Then down and down I sank from joy
To shrivelled age, though scarce a boy,
And knew for all my fear to die
That I with those lost friends should lie.

Now in slow imprisoned pain
Lie I in the garret bed,
With this crampt and weighted brain
That scarce has power to wish me fled
To burst the vault and soar away
Into the apocalypse of day,
And so regain that tingling light
That twice has passed before my sight.

[*London Mercury*, Vol. 5, No. 28, February 1922.
The Shepherd, April 1922]

from A Summer's Fancy

SOMETIMES came letters from my friend, who told
Of harvest, feast and fair, of ancient men
Dismounted, headstoned, farm and business sold,
Some lovers wed, some lost to love again;
  And, chance, his pleasant Nell would take the pen
  And bid me still be ready, and to come
A longed-for guest when our old church would make
       them bride and groom.

Through the four seasons of these happy isles
And lands beyond the changeless changing seas
Myriads like those were walking then all smiles,
Whispering their vows below moon-haunted trees,
  Listening the sureness echoing over the leas
  Of holy bells soon to be set a-ringing
For very brooks to chime and hills and vales break into
      singing.

What cloud is this amazing the good year
There was a speck on the horizon's bloom
Scarce seen, an hour ago. Now huge, now drear,
Now blasting reason, hangs the vulture gloom,
  And maniac wailings of immense simoom
  Are pouring through the universe. Arise!
The fury of the tempest War is on you. – The red dies

From cheek and lip new-vowed to love and life,
While the world plunges, and the world's youth
     goes
To meet what may be; in the roar of strife
Dreamed marriage bells are still, and no priest knows
  If ever to be heard above earth's throes.
  Then the blood flows again, the mastering mind
Burns steady in the lover marching, the lone love left
      behind.

For us, the parting under those storm-skies
Was such, and at my last yearned look of you
You would not weep, as though war's cunning eyes
Would leer to see love's tear; you lived it through.
But as the train from the darkened platform drew
Seeing you swooning to your mother's breast
I knew what love was, and was sure that man is to be
      blest.

But to my friend again. He too was gone
From love's possessing into that close haze
Of Flanders whence the voice of guns roared on
To hold love breathless and make years of days;
Month after month dragged by; his destined ways
Though neighbouring mine, not for a moment
      crossed,
Month after month we lived astonished through the
      holocaust.

Then the two friends a moment come together,
Strange luck, together, in the weary gloom
Of endless battle set to scowling weather,
Of death-in-life and unescapable doom.
As I sat drinking in an inn's thronged room
Muffled in late disaster's lingering mood,
A voice beside me shook me, there my old companion
      stood.

And then what crowded talking of the past
And with swift-flashing hope, of you, of Nell,
Of life's rewards since we had written last! –
But from such jubilant chords the song soon fell
As all our trail of terrors came to tell.
The walls about us jarred, our aching bones
Jarred to the lean long guns dragged gnashing over the
      skull-like stones.

Gun after gun, wheel after crawling wheel,
Trooped on through that ancestral rustic town,
The pale sun like a coward touched the steel,
Then hid again, again dun rain slid down,
The rocking lorries splashed the white walls brown,
And our glad meeting words, that would have flown
Home sure as weary birds, were worse moiled in war's
      monotone.

Before us both his deadly landscape spread,
The maimed land would not let us look elsewhere,
The half-shut eyes of a sweet country dead
Froze the mind's deeps with unforgettable stare.
The drumming din so barraged our career,
 Old voices but an idiot twittering seemed.
War only was; and we were war's; and all the rest
            was dreamed.

So swift the precious hour was lost while we
Called up the nightmare landmarks of the line,
The saps, the keeps, the raid's curt misery,
The roaring toppling fountain of the mine,
And miracles of crucifix or shrine
That like ourselves bad lingered on – but, sure,
All these and all must fall at last to the endless flail of war.

'Miracles never happen,' said my friend,
And 'They may happen, and they do,' said I,
'But we shall need some few before the end;
The first seven years –,' and so we put this by
And from our wine borrowed a brighter sky,
Going out thence towards the thunderous cast,
Between the lines of Flemish signs and windows trinket-
            drest.

I to my camp and he to his diverged
Where wild shells snouting up the harmless loam
Were wailing over and shouting drivers urged
Their well-loved mules ahead. – 'To all at home I'
Between ourselves and home, what leagues to come
Of calculated death in hell-fire mangling,
Of sloughs, of sleepless pangs, of Golgothas, of spirit-
            strangling.

There's the great chateau, that gray hump of stones,
And here's the church, these craters of red sludge;
His uniform hangs loose about his bones!
How scarlet's his gaped mouth! his eyes, gray
            smudge –
The frost has kept him well. See how they drudge,
A Company, poor old Sergeant Bell's a-weeping,
For half of One Platoon left in the smashed redoubt –
            they're sleeping!

Two hit, – they've surely spotted the relief;
The five-nines drop like hail, my hot scalp creeps, –
God, man, we're going out; we'll get there – if!
Down in the trench! The pouncing shrapnel sweeps
Past the bowed shoulders, fuse-caps whack the heaps
Beside, while they fight with the lapping slime,
In tears and curses towards their rest, and return in two
    days' time.

No, I'll no more of that; let that remain
Where it can never fade, being branded there
In my deep agonies; – my selfish vein
Would have it haunt those whom I hold most dear!
Forgive me that, pretend to smile, say clear,
Miracles are no legends nor decoys
Contrived in simpler days to witch the world to faith's
    employs.

For there's a wonder, that from the weary wild
Men came alive to find some first hopes crowned:
Pelion on Ossa had been easier piled
Than flesh and blood got through that woeful ground.
And happiness redoubles, that we found
My friend who thought me left in Flanders clay,
Married to Nell, and all their life promising to be May.

Their bond takes form, they will not fail, but grow
In the serenity of this rich vale,
With folks about them yet who used to show
Kindness in early days, now aged and hale:
Round the bright hearth their children will regale
Their pretty minds as with a twinkling eye
Their father tells the Homeric tales of our first liberty.

And in the round of labour and love-cheer,
There should be feasts and blithe conventicles,
The grand occasions of the rural year,
Lamb-fairs, clubs, dances, church's festivals,
And there the nation's far-heard chronicles
Will with a quiet mind be heard and weighed;
There life will be: God feared, the King honoured, the
    Law obeyed.

The cottage where those two friends live must long
Enchant the wanderer's envying eye, and ours,
And from their damson trees the blackcap's song
Will vie with the anthem of their crowding flowers;
Husbandry's glass will measure out their hours,
And every honest mind that sees their home
Will go his way refreshed with such riches in little
      room.

So may it prove! So may the nymphs that haunt
These iris'd waters, or these colonnades
Of lullabying trees, make them their chant
To the budding hearts of future youths and maids
Who shall be walking in their suns and shades;
And they shall hear, unguessing whence or how,
Sweet gusts of inward song, old fame, and wreathe glad
      vow with vow.

Over the green the hour is tolling sweet,
The hammers clink in the forge, the children run
From school with shrill delight down sleepy street:
There where the last wall's pear-tree takes the sun
See the red bonnets and blue caps come on.
The wide lea surely gleams more as they pass,
And it is earth-born joy that's whispering through the
      tall white grass.

That hour-bell rings to tell me, I must leave
Once more the world that housed me homely of old,
But this day's parting shall not make me grieve,
Love's joy increases joy a hundredfold.
For one flower withered, look, what hosts unfold!
May I then part contented at dewfall
Having one theme that passes this, if you will tune it all.

'A Summer's Fancy' was written in 1922 in 'the spare port cabin' of S.S. *Trefusis*, a cargo ship bound for Bahia Blanca: and has subsequently been revised. ('Preface', *Poems 1930-1940*, p. viii.)

[*A Summer's Fancy*, November 1930]

The Brook

UP, my jewel! let's away
    There where none but young love lingers;
Bells are ringing folks to pray,
    But ours are older bells and ringers,
Where the stream's broken gleams
    Glance through tresses of green willow,
Fishes glide, and beside
    Flowers laugh, blue, white and yellow.

On this bridge 'tis good to lean,
    Cooling care with the dance and dripple,
Nor do you your lovelight screen
    But outgleam the dimpling ripple:
Minim waves, nutshell caves,
    Cataracts over pebbles hurling,
To whose falls on the walls
    Myriad mimic suns go twirling!

But what dying dying fall,
    What low ebbing syllables
Hear I now? what ghosts recall
    Their shadowing piteous chronicles?
O my dear! this pale fear –
    Sun so cold, so dark! O never –
My life stream's broken gleams
    Stolen into the gulf for ever!

A fancy; but like some of the others it reveals that I was somewhat ill for a few years after war I.

[*Nation & Athenaeum*, 25 March 1922
To Nature, June 1923]

Water Moment

THE silver eel slips through the waving weeds,
And in the tunnelled shining stone recedes,
The earnest eye surveys the crystal pond
And guards the cave: the sweet shoals pass beyond.
The watery jewels that these have for eyes,
The tiger streaks in him that hind most plies,
The red gold wings that smooth their darting paces,
The sunlight dancing about their airs and graces,
Burn that strange watcher's heart; then the sly brain
Speaks, all the dumb shoal shrieks, and by the stone
The silver death writhes with the chosen one.

[*London Mercury*, Vol. 37, No. 264, January 1923
To Nature, June 1923]

The Self-Imprisoned

O THE days when I was young!
'Tis the never-silent cry.
But it cannot still my tongue
That I've paid so many a sigh
For the days when I was young and the merry hope gone by.

Shall I shame to cry out loud
What all that's born must say, –
O the pity that the proud
Sweet morning's died away
And one that soared to the cloud goes a-grovelling through the
    day?

My sense so dulled scarce hears
The quick song of the past,
Scarce copies those angel years –
They are ghosts and flitter fast;
Their smiles but wake new tears, their radiance leaves me aghast.

90

Nature's inns and resting-places –
Kind is every oak and pine;
Kind the flashing runlet's faces,
Kind the flower's coquetting shine.
Truly life's not lost her graces, – but I have murdered mine.

[*To Nature*, June 1923]

The Still Hour

AS in the silent darkening room I lay,
While winter's early evening, heavy-paced
As ploughmen from our swarthy soil, groped on
From the cold mill upon the horizon hill
And over paddocks to the neighbouring lodges
And lay as I, tired out with colourless toil,
Inert, the lubber fiend, whose puffing drowse
The moon's dawn scarce would fret, through the low cloud, –
When thus at ebb I lay, my silence flowered
Gently as later bloom into a warm
Harmonious chiming; like a listener I
Was hushed. The spirits of remembrance all
With one consent made music, a flood, a haze,
A vista all to one ripe blushing blended.

That summer veil of sweet sound then awhile
Gave me clear voices, as though from rosy distance
There had been drifting multitude of song,
And then the bells each in his round were heard;
The tower that throned them seen, and even the golden
Chanticleer that frolicked on its top.
From my broad murmuring ode there came fair forth
The cries of playing children on one day,
At one blue dewy hour, by one loved green;
And then the brook was tumbling lit like gems
Down its old sluice, and old boy-heroes stood
To catch its sparkling stonefish – I heard even
The cry that hailed the chestnut tench's downfall
In the next swim, that strange historic victim.
From church and pasture, sweetheart and sworn friend,
From the hill's hopgrounds to the lowest leas
In the rook-routed vale, from the blind boy

91

Who lived by me to the dwellers in the heath,
From robins building in the gipsy's kettle
Thrown in our hedge, to waterfowl above
The mouldering mill, distinct and happy now
Ten thousand singings from my childhood rang.

And time seemed stealing forward as they sounded,
The syllables of first delights passed; years
That ended childhood with their secret sigh
Uttered their joys, still longed-for, still enshrined.
And then what voices? Straight, it seemed, from those,
While a long age was silent as the grave,
The utterance passed to that stern course of chances
That crowded far-off Flanders with ourselves.
I heard the signallers lead the strong battalion
With bold songs flying to the breeze like banners,
The quiet courage once again of Daniells
By some few words built up a fort around me,
And while the long guns clattered through the towns
I, rather, heard the clack of market-women,
The hostel's gramophone and gay girls fooling,
And chants in painted churches, and my friend's
Lively review of Flemish contraries.
Or, was not this the green Bethune canal
And these our shouts, our laughs, our awkward plunges,
While summer's day went cloudless to its close?
There shone the Ancre, red-leafed woods above it,
The blue speed of its waters swirled through causeways;
There from his hammock in the apple orchard
Up sprang old Swain and rallied intruding youngsters.
The company now fell in, to the very yard,
And once again marched eager towards the Somme,
And there, a score of voices leapt again
After a hare that left her seat in the corn.
I think I'd know that twinkling field to-day.

So in a swift succession my still hour
Heard Flanders voices, in the line direct
From those of childhood; but at last the host
In such confusion as nigh stopt my breath
With glory and anguish striving, drew far on
And all became a drone, that in decline
From summer's bravery changed to autumn chill,
And as the music vague and piteous grew,
I saw the mist die from its pleasant charm,

Now fierce with early frost its numb shroud lay
Along sad ridges, and as one aloof
I saw the praying rockets mile on mile
Climb all too weak from those entangled there
Climb for the help that could not help them there;
And even these purple vapours died away
And left the surly evening brown as clay
Upon those ridges battered into chaos
Whence one deep moaning, one deep moaning came.

Swain, M.C. was our Captain Quartermaster, but in the March Offensive of 1918
was Adjutant & killed. A character! unfrightenable.

[*The Adelphi*, Vol. 1, No. 7, December 1923
To Nature, June 1923]

The Aftermath

SWIFT away the century flies,
    Time has yet the wind for wings,
In the past the midnight lies;
    But my morning never springs.

Who goes there? come, ghost or man,
    You were with us, you will know;
Let us commune, there's no ban
    On speech for us if we speak low.

Time has healed the wound, they say,
    Gone's the weeping and the rain;
Yet you and I suspect, the day
    Will never be the same again.

Is it day? I thought there crept
    Some frightened pale rays through the fog,
And where the lank black ash-trees wept
    I thought the birds were just agog.

But no, this fiction died before
    The swirling gloom, as soon as seen;
The thunder's brow, the thunder's roar,
    Darkness that's felt strode swift between.

O euphrasy for ruined eyes!
   I chose, it seemed, a flowering thorn;
The white blooms were but brazen lies,
   The tree I looked upon was torn

In snarling lunacy of pain,
   A brown charred trunk that deadly cowered,
And when I stared across the plain
   Where once the gladdening green hill towered,

It shone a second, then the greed
   Of death had fouled it; dark it stood,
A hump of wilderness untreed
   Where the kind Dove would never brood.

[*To Nature*, June 1923]

UNDERTONES OF WAR

A House in Festubert

WITH blind eyes meeting the mist and moon
And yet with blossoming trees robed round,
With gashes black, nay, one great wound,
Amazing still it stands its ground;
    Sad soul, here stay you.

It held, one time, such happy hours,
Its tables shone with smiles and filled
The hungry – Home! 'twas theirs, is ours,
We house it here and laugh unkilled.
    Hoarse gun, now, pray you –

It knew the hand and voice of Sleep,
Sleep was its friend and nightly came,
And still the bony laths would keep
One friendship, but poor Sleep's gone lame.
    O poisoner, Mahu!

A hermit might have built a cell
Among those evergreens, beside
That mellow wall: they serve as well
For four lean guns. Soft, hermits, hide,
    Lest pride display you.

It hived the bird's call, the bee's hum,
The sunbeams crossing the garden's shade –
So fond of summer! still they come,
But steel-born bees, birds, beams invade.
    – Could summer betray you?

Mahu! The Prince of Darkness is a Gentleman, Mahu he's called, and Modo. –
Edgar in *King Lear*.

[*Undertones of War*, November 1928]

The Sentry's Mistake*

THE chapel at the crossways bore no scar,
Nor near had whining covey of shells yet pounced,
The calm saints in the chapel knew no war,
No meaning there the horizon's roars announced;
    We halted, and were glad; the country lay
    After our marching like a sabbath day.

Round the still quadrangle of the empty farm
The company soon had settled their new home;
The cherry-boughs were beckoning every arm,
The stream ran wrinkling by with playful foam,
    And when the guard was at the gateway set,
    Surrounding pastoral sweetly stole their wit.

So out upon the road, gamekeeper-like,
The cowman now turned warrior measured out
His up-and-down sans cursed bundook and spike,
Under his arm a cudgel brown and stout;
    An air of comfort and kind ownership,
    A philosophic smile upon his lip.

For it seemed sin to soil the harmonious air
With the parade of weapons built to kill.
But now a flagged car came ill-omened there.
The crimson-mottled monarch, shocked and shrill,
    Sent our poor sentry scampering for his gun,
    Made him once more "the terror of the Hun."

Richebourg St. Vaast. And damned me, though I believe Lytton was quite willing
to let our guard be armed with a stick. In those days we did not think of Germans
much. [Titled 'The Guard's Mistake' in *Undertones of War*.]

[*Masks of Time*, June 1925
Undertones of War, November 1928]

Two Voices

"THERE'S something in the air," he said
   In the large parlour cool and bare;
The plain words in his hearers bred
   A tumult, yet in silence there
All waited; wryly gay, he left the phrase,
Ordered the march and bade us go our ways.

"We're going South, man"; as he spoke
   The howitzer with huge ping-bang
Racked the light hut; as thus he broke
   The death-news, bright the skylarks sang;
He took his riding-crop and humming went
Among the apple-trees all bloom and scent.

Now far withdraws the roaring night
   Which wrecked our flower after the first
Of those two voices; misty light
   Shrouds Thiepval Wood and all its worst:
But still "There's something in the air" I hear,
And still "We're going South, man," deadly near.

At Hinges near Lacoutre. He: Capt. Wallace, our Adjutant. 'King Edward's Road'?
Before the march to the Somme. [Formerly 'The Survivors' (1916).]

[*Weekly Westminster*, 2 August 1924
Masks of Time, June 1925
Undertones of War, November 1928]

Illusions

TRENCHES in the moonlight, in the lulling moonlight
Have had their loveliness; when dancing dewy grasses
Caressed us passing along their earthy lanes;
When the crucifix hanging over was strangely illumined,
And one imagined music, one even heard the brave bird
In the sighing orchards flute above the weedy well.
There are such moments; forgive me that I note them,

Nor gloze that there comes soon the nemesis of beauty,
In the fluttering relics that at first glimmer wakened
Terror – the no-man's ditch suddenly forking:
There, the enemy's best with bombs and brains and courage!
– Softly, swiftly, at once be animal and angel –
But O no, no, they're Death's malkins dangling in the wire
    For the moon's interpretation.

Richebourg & Cuinchy. A patrol. Unstead was with me, and May, and Bodle.
Richebourg l'Avué. June 1916.

[*Poetica*, Vol. [1], No. 3, April 1925
Undertones of War, November 1928 (revised)]

Premature Rejoicing*

WHAT'S that over there?
                    Thiepval Wood.
Take a steady look at it; it'll do you good.
Here, these glasses will help you. See any flowers?
There sleeps Titania (correct – the Wood is ours);
There sleeps Titania in a deep dugout,
Waking, she wonders what all the din's about,
And smiles through her tears, and looks ahead ten years,
And sees her Wood again, and her usual Grenadiers,
    All in green,
    Music in the moon;
  That burnt rubbish you've just seen
  Won't beat the Fairy Queen;
    All the same, it's a shade too soon
    For you to scribble rhymes
    In your army book
    About those times;
    Take another look;
  That's where the difficulty is, over there.

Illustrates my meetings with Realists in August 1916.

[*Poems 1914-30*, December 1930]

Escape

A Colonel:
> THERE are four officers, this message says,
> Lying all dead at Mesnil.
> One shell pitched clean amongst 'em at the foot
> Of Jacob's Ladder. They're all Sussex men.
> I fear poor Flood and Warne were of that party.
> And the Brigade wants them identified ...

A Mind:
> Now God befriend me,
> The next word not send me
> To view those ravished trunks
> And hips and blackened hunks.

A Colonel:
> No, not you, Bunny, you've just now come down.
> I've something else for you.
> > Orderly!
> > > (*Sir!*)
> Find Mr. Wrestman.

Caldwell had the job, I believe. He had done less than the others, but this must have made up the deficit. Barrow and Johns were probably two of the dead. It was just before September the Third I think. Mesnil – a terror.

[*Mask of Time*, June 1925
Undertones of War, November 1928]

Preparations for Victory

> MY soul, dread not the pestilence that hags
> The valley; flinch not you, my body young,
> At these great shouting smokes and snarling jags
> Of fiery iron; as yet may not be flung
> The dice that claims you. Manly move among
> These ruins, and what you must do, do well;
> Look, here are gardens, there mossed boughs are hung

99

With apples whose bright cheeks none might excel,
And there's a house as yet unshattered by a shell.

"I'll do my best," the soul makes sad reply,
"And I will mark the yet unmurdered tree,
The relics of dear homes that court the eye,
And yet I see them not as I would see.
Hovering between, a ghostly enemy
Sickens the light, and poisoned, withered, wan,
The least defiled turns desperate to me."
The body, poor unpitied Caliban,
Parches and sweats and grunts to win the name of Man.

Days or eternities like swelling waves
Surge on, and still we drudge in this dark maze,
The bombs and coils and cans by strings of slaves
Are borne to serve the coming day of days;
Pale sleep in slimy cellars scarce allays
With its brief blank the burden. Look, we lose;
The sky is gone, the lightless drenching haze
Of rainstorm chills the bone; earth, air are foes,
The black fiend leaps brick-red as life's last picture goes.

Hamel on the Ancre in the days preceding our attack on the Beaumont ridge, 3 Sept. 1916.

[*Masks of Time*, 1925
Undertones of War, November 1928]

Zero

O ROSY red, O torrent splendour
    Staining all the Orient gloom,
O celestial work of wonder –
    A million mornings in one bloom!

What, does the artist of creation
    Try some new plethora of flame,
For his eye's fresh fascination?
    Has the old cosmic fire grown tame?

In what subnatural strange awaking
    Is this body, which seems mine?

These feet towards that blood-burst making,
    These ears which thunder, these hands which twine

On grotesque iron? Icy-clear
    The air of a mortal day shocks sense,
My shaking men pant after me here.
    The acid vapours hovering dense,

The fury whizzing in dozens down,
    The clattering rafters, clods calcined,
The blood in the flints and the trackway brown –
    I see I am clothed and in my right mind;

The dawn but hangs behind the goal.
    What is that artist's joy to me?
Here limps poor Jock with a gash in the poll,
    His red blood now is the red I see,

The swooning white of him, and that red!
    These bombs in boxes, the craunch of shells,
The second-hand flitting round; ahead!
    It's plain we were born for this, naught else.

Worley's expression. [Refers to *Undertones of War* title 'Come On, My Lucky Lads']
September 3rd 1916. The first moments of the attack at Hamel. [Later 'Zero, 1916']

[*Masks of Time*, June 1925
Undertones of War, November 1928]

At Senlis Once

O HOW comely it was and how reviving,
When with clay and with death no longer striving
    Down firm roads we came to houses
    With women chattering and green grass thriving.

Now though rains in a cataract descended,
We could glow, with our tribulation ended –
    Count not days, the present only
    Was thought of, how could it ever be expended?

Clad so cleanly, this remnant of poor wretches
Picked up life like the hens in orchard ditches,

Gazed on the mill-sails, heard the church-bell,
Found an honest glass all manner of riches.

How they crowded the barn with lusty laughter,
Hailed the pierrots and shook each shadowy rafter,
Even could ridicule their own sufferings,
Sang as though nothing but joy came after!

Senlis was a village of a few hundred people only. Our stay there was cut short. It
was a damp gloomy day or two, when the thatch and plaster all seemed mouldy –
and yet ...

[*Masks of Time*, June 1925
Undertones of War, November 1928]

Into the Salient

SALLOWS like heads in Polynesia,
With few and blood-stuck hairs,
Mud-layered cobble-stones,
Soldiers in smoky sheds, blackening uniforms and walls with their
    cookery;
Shell-holes in roofs, in roads,
Even in advertisements
Of bicycles and beer;
The Middle Ages gone to sleep, and woken up to this –
A salvo, four flat slamming explosions.
When you come out the wrong side of the ruin, you are facing Hill
    Sixty,
Hill Sixty is facing you.
You have been planted on the rim of a volcano,
Which will bring forth its fruit – at any second.
Better to be shielded from these facts;
There is a cellar, or was just now.
If the wreck isn't knocked in on us all,
We may emerge past the two Belgian policemen,
The owners' representatives,
Standing in their capes on the steps of the hollow estaminet
Open at all hours to all the winds
At the Poperinghe end of Ypres.
O if we do, if time will pass in time,
We will march
With rifles butt-upwards, in our teeth, any way you like,
Into seven days of country where you come out any door.

We went north into the Ypres salient & town, and it was a little time before we knew how overlooked by the German positions every place was.

[*Poems 1914-30*, December 1930]

The Zonnebeke Road

MORNING, if this late withered light can claim
Some kindred with that merry flame
Which the young day was wont to fling through space!
Agony stares from each gray face.
And yet the day is come; stand down! stand down!
Your hands unclasp from rifles while you can,
The frost has pierced them to the bended bone?
Why, see old Stevens there, that iron man,
Melting the ice to shave his grotesque chin:
Go ask him, shall we win?
I never liked this bay, some foolish fear
Caught me the first time that I came in here;
That dugout fallen in awakes, perhaps,
Some formless haunting of some corpse's chaps.
True, and wherever we have held the line,
There were such corners, seeming-saturnine
For no good cause.
           Now where Haymarket starts,
That is no place for soldiers with weak hearts;
The minenwerfers have it to the inch.
Look, how the snow-dust whisks along the road,
Piteous and silly; the stones themselves must flinch
In this east wind; the low sky like a load
Hangs over – a dead-weight. But what a pain
Must gnaw where its clay cheek
Crushes the shell-chopped trees that fang the plain –
The ice-bound throat gulps out a gargoyle shriek.
The wretched wire before the village line
Rattles like rusty brambles or dead bine,
And then the daylight oozes into dun;
Black pillars, those are trees where roadways run.
Even Ypres now would warm our souls; fond fool,
Our tour's but one night old, seven more to cool!
O screaming dumbness, O dull clashing death,
Shreds of dead grass and willows, homes and men,

103

Watch as you will, men clench their chattering teeth
And freeze you back with that one hope, disdain.

Hard weather: Potijze trenches, and they were poor.

[*Masks of Time*, June 1925
Undertones of War, November 1928]

Trench Raid near Hooge

AT an hour before the rosy-fingered
    Morning should come
To wonder again what meant these sties,
These wailing shots, these glaring eyes,
    These moping mum,

Through the black reached strange long rosy fingers
    All at one aim
Protending, and bending: down they swept,
Successions of similars after leapt
    And bore red flame

To one small ground of the eastern distance,
    And thunderous touched.
East then and west false dawns fan-flashed
And shut, and gaped; false thunders clashed.
    Who stood and watched

Caught piercing horror from the desperate pit
    Which with ten men
Was centre of this. The blood burnt, feeling
The fierce truth there and the last appealing,
    "Us? Us? Again?"

Nor rosy dawn at last appearing
    Through the icy shade
Might mark without trembling the new deforming
Of earth that had seemed past further storming.
    Her fingers played,

One thought, with something of human pity
    On six or seven

Whose looks were hard to understand,
But that they ceased to care what hand
Lit earth and heaven.

Seen as it happened by J.G.W. Clarke and E.B. on their dark walk round. We were raided on the railway line at Potijze, but I was thinking also of another raid I could see from my tour at Zillebeke.

[*Poetica*, Vol. [1], No. 3, April 1925
Undertones of War, November 1928 (revised)]

Concert Party: Busseboom

THE stage was set, the house was packed,
    The famous troop began;
Our laughter thundered, act by act;
    Time light as sunbeams ran.

Dance sprang and spun and neared and fled,
    Jest chirped at gayest pitch,
Rhythm dazzled, action sped
    Most comically rich.

With generals and lame privates both
    Such charms worked wonders, till
The show was over – lagging loth
    We faced the sunset chill;

And standing on the sandy way,
    With the cracked church peering past,
We heard another matinée,
    We heard the maniac blast

Of barrage south by Saint Eloi,
    And the red lights flaming there
Called madness: Come, my bonny boy,
    And dance to the latest air.

To this new concert, white we stood;
    Cold certainty held our breath;
While men in the tunnels below Larch Wood
    Were kicking men to death.

47th Division Revue. That was as it actually happened, on an early spring morning in 1917, – the 47th Division I think gave the Revue, in a large hut not far from Vlamertinghe.

[*Undertones of War*, November 1928]

Rural Economy (1917)

THERE was winter in those woods,
    And still it was July:
There were Thule solitudes
    With thousands huddling nigh;
There the fox had left his den,
The scraped holes hid not stoats but men.

To these woods the rumour teemed
    Of peace five miles away;
In sight, hills hovered, houses gleamed
    Where last perhaps we lay
Till the cockerels bawled bright morning and
The hours of life slipped the slack hand.

In sight, life's farms sent forth their gear;
    Here rakes and ploughs lay still;
Yet, save some curious clods, all here
    Was raked and ploughed with a will.
The sower was the ploughman too,
And iron seeds broadcast he threw.

What husbandry could outdo this?
    With flesh and blood he fed
The planted iron that nought amiss
    Grew thick and swift and red,
And in a night though ne'er so cold
Those acres bristled a hundredfold.

Why, even the wood as well as field
    This ruseful farmer knew
Could be reduced to plough and tilled,
    And if he planned, he'd do;
The field and wood, all bone-fed loam,
Shot up a roaring harvest-home.

106

Observatory Ridge, looking backwards towards Scherpenberg.

[*Nation & Athenaeum*, 4 November 1922
To Nature, June 1923
Undertones of War, November 1928]

E.W.T.: on the death of his Betty

AND she is gone, whom, dream or truth,
You lived for in this wreck of youth,
   And on your brow sits age,
   Who's quickly won his siege.

My friend, you will not wish a word
Of striven help in this worst gird
   Of fortune as she gets
   From us our race's debts.

I see you with this subtlest blow
Like a stunned man softly go;
   Then you, love-baffled boy,
   Smile with a mournful joy.

Thereat I read, you plainly know
The time draws near when the fierce foe
   Shall your poor body tear
   And mix with mud and air.

Your smile is borne in that foredoom,
Beaten, you see your victory bloom,
   And fortune cheats her end,
   And death draws nigh, a friend.

At Zudausques. Ernest Tice, a Christ's Hospital boy, killed 31 July.

[*Masks of Time*, June 1925
Undertones of War, November 1928]

Battalion in Rest

SOME found an owl's nest in the hollow skull
Of the first pollard from the malthouse wall;
   Some hurried through the swarming sedge
   About the ballast-pond's bright edge,
And flashed through sunny deeps like boys from school;
All was discovery, love and laughter all.

The girls along the dykes of those moist miles
Went on raft boats to take their cows afield,
   And eyes from many an English farm
   Saw and owned the mode had charm;
One well might mark the silence and the smiles;
With such sweet balms, our wounds must soon be healed.

The jovial sun sprang up as bright each day
As fancy's sun could be, and climbed, heaven's youth,
   To make the marching mornings cheat
   Still-hectoring Mars of his receipt –
Who cannot hear the songs that led the way,
See the trim companies with their eyes on truth?

At evening, by the lonely white-walled house,
Where Que-C'est-Drôle and Mon-Dieu stole to glance,
   One bold platoon all turned to players
   With masquerade and strumming airs;
The short clown darted nimble as a mouse,
The tambourine tapped out the stiff-stepped dance.

A shadowed corner suddenly found voice
As in the dusk I passed; it bade me stay.
   The bottle to my lips was raised –
   God help us, Serjeant, I was mazed
By that sharp fire your wine – but I rejoice!
Could I but meet you again at the end o' the day!

Not seldom, soft by meadows deep in dew,
Another lit my soul with his calm shine.
   There were cadences and whispers
   In his ways that made my vespers –

A night-piece fitting well that temple blue
Where stars new trembled with delight's design.

[Against lines 17-18] L/c Tanner & the other signallers, very inventive of a ballad.
[Against line 21] Salter's company: B platoon.
[Against line 28] Ashford.
[Against line 32] Naylor.
Houlle & Moulle. Sergeant Ashford, and H.C. Naylor our young architect and
idealist. [Later 'Battalion in Rest, July 1917'.]

[*Poetica*, Vol. [1], No. 3, April 1925
Masks of Time, June 1925 (revised)
Undertones of War, November 1928]

Vlamertinghe: Passing the Chateau, July 1917

"AND all her silken flanks with garlands drest" –
But we are coming to the sacrifice.
Must those have flowers who are not yet gone West?
May those have flowers who live with death and lice?
This must be the floweriest place
That earth allows; the queenly face
Of the proud mansion borrows grace for grace
Spite of those brute guns lowing at the skies.

Bold great daisies, golden lights,
Bubbling roses' pinks and whites –
Such a gay carpet! poppies by the million;
Such damask! such vermilion!
But if you ask me, mate, the choice of colour
Is scarcely right; this red should have been much duller.

It was still a fine-looking Château, with a 12-inch battery close to the front view.

[*Undertones of War*, November 1928]

Third Ypres

TRIUMPH! How strange, how strong had triumph come
On weary hate of foul and endless war
When from its grey gravecloths awoke anew
The summer day. Among the tumbled wreck
Of fascined lines and mounds the light was peering,
Half-smiling upon us, and our newfound pride;
The terror of the waiting night outlived,
The time too crowded for the heart to count
All the sharp cost in friends killed on the assault.
No hook of all the octopus had held us,
Here stood we trampling down the ancient tyrant.
So shouting dug we among the monstrous pits.

Amazing quiet fell upon the waste,
Quiet intolerable to those who felt
The hurrying batteries beyond the masking hills
For their new parley setting themselves in array
In crafty fourms unmapped.
                    No, these, smiled faith,
Are dumb for the reason of their overthrow.
They move not back, they lie among the crews
Twisted and choked, they'll never speak again.
Only the copse where once might stand a shrine
Still clacked and suddenly hissed its bullets by.
The War would end, the Line was on the move,
And at a bound the impassable was passed.
We lay and waited with extravagant joy.

Now dulls the day and chills; comes there no word
From those who swept through our new lines to flood
The lines beyond? but little comes, and so
Sure as a runner time himself's accosted.
And the slow moments shake their heavy heads,
And croak, "They're done, they'll none of them get through,
They're done, they've all died on the entanglements,
The wire stood up like an unplashed hedge and thorned
With giant spikes – and there they've paid the bill."

Then comes the black assurance, then the sky's
Mute misery lapses into trickling rain,

That wreathes and swims and soon shuts in our world.
And those distorted guns, that lay past use,
Why – miracles not over! – all a-firing!
The rain's no cloak from their sharp eyes. And you,
Poor signaller, you I passed by this emplacement,
You whom I warned, poor daredevil, waving your flags,
Amid this screeching I pass you again and shudder
At the lean green flies upon the red flesh madding.
Runner, stand by a second. Your message. – He's gone,
Falls on a knee, and his right hand uplifted
Claws his last message from his ghostly enemy,
Turns stone-like. Well I liked him, that young runner,
But there's no time for that. O now for the word
To order us flash from these drowning roaring traps
And even hurl upon that snarling wire?
Why are our guns so impotent?

                               The grey rain,
Steady as the sand in an hourglass on this day,
Where through the window the red lilac looks,
And all's so still, the chair's odd click is noise –
The rain is all heaven's answer, and with hearts
Past reckoning we are carried into night
And even sleep is nodding here and there.

The second night steals through the shrouding rain.
We in our numb thought crouching long have lost
The mockery triumph, and in every runner
Have urged the mind's eye see the triumph to come,
The sweet relief, the straggling out of hell
Into whatever burrows may be given
For life's recall. Then the fierce destiny speaks.
This was the calm, we shall look back for this.
The hour is come; come, move to the relief!
Dizzy we pass the mule-strewn track where once
The ploughman whistled as he loosed his team;
And where he turned home-hungry on the road,
The leaning pollard marks us hungrier turning,
We crawl to save the remnant who have torn
Back from the tentacled wire, those whom no shell
Has charred into black carcasses – Relief!
They grate their teeth until we take their room,
And through the churn of moonless night and mud
And flaming burst and sour gas we are huddled
Into the ditches where they bawl sense awake

111

And in a frenzy that none could reason calm,
(Whimpering some, and calling on the dead)
They turn away: as in a dream they find
Strength in their feet to bear back that strange whim
Their body.
                At the noon of the dreadful day
Our trench and death's is on a sudden stormed
With huge and shattering salvoes, the clay dances
In founts of clods around the concrete sties,
Where still the brain devises some last armour
To live out the poor limbs.
                      This wrath's oncoming
Found four of us together in a pillbox,
Skirting the abyss of madness with light phrases,
White and blinking, in false smiles grimacing.
The demon grins to see the game, a moment
Passes, and – still the drum-tap dongs my brain
To a whirring void – through the great breach above me
The light comes in with icy shock and the rain
Horridly drops. Doctor, talk, talk! if dead
Or stunned I know not; the stinking powdered concrete,
The lyddite turns me sick – my hair's all full
Of this smashed concrete. O I'll drag you, friends,
Out of the sepulchre into the light of day,
For this is day, the pure and sacred day.
And while I squeak and gibber over you,
Look, from the wreck a score of field-mice nimble,
And tame and curious look about them; (these
Calmed me, on these depended my salvation).

There comes my sergeant, and by all the powers
The wire is holding to the right battalion,
And I can speak – but I myself first spoken
Hear a known voice now measured even to madness
Call me by name.
                "For God's sake send and help us,
Here in a gunpit, all headquarters done for,
Forty or more, the nine-inch came right through,
All splashed with arms and legs, and I myself
The only one not killed, not even wounded.
You'll send – God bless you!" The more monstrous fate
Shadows our own, the mind swoons doubly burdened,
Taught how for miles our anguish groans and bleeds,
A whole sweet countryside amuck with murder;
Each moment puffed into a year with death.

Still swept the rain, roared guns,
Still swooped into the swamps of flesh and blood,
All to the drabness of uncreation sunk,
And all thought dwindled to a moan, Relieve!
But who with what command can now relieve
The dead men from that chaos, or my soul?

July 31, 1917 & the next day or two.

[*The Shepherd*, April 1922
Undertones of War, November 1928]

Pillbox

JUST see what's happening, Worley! – Worley rose
And round the angled doorway thrust his nose
And Serjeant Hoad went too to snuff the air.
Then war brought down his fist, and missed the pair!
Yet Hoad was scratched by a splinter, the blood came,
And out burst terrors that he'd striven to tame,
A good man, Hoad, for weeks. *I'm blown to bits*,
He groans, he screams. *Come, Bluffer, where's your wits?*
Says Worley, *Bluffer, you've a blighty, man!*
All in the pillbox urged him, here began
His freedom: *Think of Eastbourne and your dad.*
The poor man lay at length and brief and mad
Flung out his cry of doom; soon ebbed and dumb
He yielded. Worley with a tot of rum
And shouting in his face could not restore him.
The ship of Charon over channel bore him.
All marvelled even on that most deathly day
To see this life so spirited away.

Sept. 29, 1917. Tower Hamlets, Menin Rd. Again, the Menin Rd. 'do'. We were in captured pillboxes & c.

[*Masks of Time*, June 1925
Undertones of War, November 1928]

The Welcome

HE'D scarcely come from leave and London,
Still was carrying a leather case,
When he surprised Headquarters pillbox
And sat down sweating in the filthy place.

He was a tall, lean, pale-looked creature,
With nerves that seldom ceased to wince,
Past war had long preyed on his nature,
And war had doubled in horror since.

There was a lull, the adjutant even
Came to my hole: You cheerful sinner,
If nothing happens till half-past seven,
Come over then, we're going to have dinner.

Back he went with his fierce red head;
We were sourly canvassing his jauntiness, when
Something happened at Headquarters pillbox.
"Don't go there," cried one of my men.

The shell had struck right into the doorway,
The smoke lazily floated away;
There were six men in that concrete doorway,
Now a black muckheap blocked the way.

Inside, one who had scarcely shaken
The air of England out of his lungs
Was alive, and sane; it shall be spoken
While any of those who were there have tongues.

Tower Hamlets. In the smaller battle of the Menin Rd. at the end of Sept. 1917.

[*Masks of Time*, June 1925
Undertones of War, November 1928]

Gouzeaucourt: The Deceitful Calm

HOW unpurposed, how inconsequential
Seemed those southern lines when in the pallor
   Of the dying winter
   First we went there!

Grass thin-waving in the wind approached them,
Red roofs in the near view feigned survival,
   Lovely mockers, when we
   There took over.

There war's holiday seemed, nor though at known times
Gusts of flame and jingling steel descended
   On the bare tracks, would you
   Picture death there.

Snow or rime-frost made a solemn silence,
Bluish darkness wrapped in dangerous safety;
   Old hands thought of tidy
   Living-trenches!

There it was, my dears, that I departed,
Scarce a plainer traitor ever! There too
   Many of you soon paid for
   That false mildness.

We were taken out of the Passchendaele battle, at least out of the intolerable business of holding the ground taken, in Jan. 1918, and went down to the 5th Army Front which was to be overrun by the Germans on 21 March.

[*Undertones of War*, November 1928]

DELAYED ACTIONS

The Prophet

IT is a country,
Says this old guide-book to the Netherlands,
– Written when Waterloo was hardly over,
And justified "a warmer interest
In English travellers" – Flanders is a country
Which, boasting not "so many natural beauties"
As others, yet has history enough.
I like the book; it flaunts the polished phrase
Which our forefathers practised equally
To bury admirals or sell beaver hats;
Let me go on, and note you here and there
Words with a difference to the likes of us.
The author "will not dwell on the temptations
Which many parts of Belgium offer"; he
"Will not insist on the salubrity
Of the air." I thank you, sir, for those few words.
With which we find ourselves in sympathy.
And here are others: "here the unrivalled skill
Of British generals, and the British soldier's
Unconquerable valour ..." no, not us.
Proceed.
"The necessary cautions on the road" ...
Gas helmets at the alert, no daylight movement?
"But lately much attention has been paid
To the coal mines." Amen, roars many a fosse
Down south, and slag-heap unto slag-heap calls.
"The Flemish farmers are likewise distinguished
For their attention to manure." Perchance.
First make your mixen, then about it raise
Your tenements; let the house and sheds and sties
And arch triumphal opening on the mud
Inclose that Mecca in a square. The fields,
Our witness saith, are for the most part small,

117

And "leases are unfortunately short."
In this again perceive veracity;
At Zillebeke the cultivator found
That it was so; and Fritz, who thought to settle
Down by Verbrandenmolen, came with spades,
And dropped his spades, and ran more dead than alive.
Nor, to disclose a secret, do I languish
For lack of a long lease on Pilkem Ridge.

While in these local hints, I cannot wait
But track the author on familiar ground.
He comes from Menin, names the village names
That since rang round the world, leaves Zillebeke,
Crosses a river (so he calls that blood-leat
Bassevillebeek), a hill (a hideous hill),
And reaches Ypres, "pleasant, well-built town."
My Belgian Traveller, did no threatening whisper
Sigh to you from the hid profound of fate
Ere you passed thence, and noted "Poperinghe.
Traffic in serge and hops"? (The words might still
Convey sound fact. Perhaps some dim hush envoy
Entered your spirit when at Furnes you wrote,
"The air is reckoned unhealthy here for strangers."
I find your pen, as driven by irony's fingers,
Defend the incorrectness of your map
With this: it was not fitting to delay,
Though "in a few weeks a new treaty of Paris
Would render it useless." Good calm worthy man,
I leave you changing horses, and I wish you
Good *blanc* at Nieuport. – Truth did not disdain
This sometime seer, crass but Cassandra-like.

[Against lines 27-28] Wants a line by Wm. Cobbett.
[Against line 38] In the attack on Larch Wood, mentioned on p. 281 [of *Undertones of War*]. Written after the war, but as from 1917.

[*Masks of Time*, June 1925
Undertones of War, November 1928]

II Peter ii 22

HARK, the new year succeeds the dead,
The bells make haste, the news is spread;
    And day by day
    "Farther away,"
"Farther away" tolls through my head.

Here slinking Slyness rules the roost
And brags and pimps, as he was used
    Before the day
    Now far away
Saw him to's puny self reduced.

And Quarrel with her hissing tongue
And hen's eye gobbles gross along
    To snap that prey
    That marched away
To save her carcass, better hung.

Come, infant Hour, though much I fear
Thy bright will shew more blackly clear
    How day by day
    Far fade away
The heights which crowned a deadlier year.

Written in despondency in a Suffolk village. Alas, returning to ordinary life had
its disillusions.

[*Mask of Time*, June 1925
Undertones of War, November 1928]

Recognition

OLD friend, I know you line by line,
    The touch, the tone, the turn of phrase,
Old autumn day, beloved and mine,
    Returning after many days;
The ten years' journey since we bade farewell
No hinted change or loss in you would ever tell.

Your countenance still ripe and kind
   Gazes upon me, godlike day,
And finding you again I find
   The tricks of time all thrown away.
The recollected turns to here and now
Beneath the equipoising glory of your brow.

Now to your Heaven the gossamers gleam,
   Still soaring in their trembling play,
Their rosy scarves are spied astream;
   Whence borne and blown no one could say –
All out and dancing in the blue profound,
The tranquil ultimation of the ages round.

And here's that narrow orchard's grass,
   The last green luck for many a mile;
The patient lines of mules I pass,
   And then must stand and talk awhile
With gallant Maycock, spurred and gaitered, glowing
With this ripe sun, and red as any orchard growing.

This comrade, born to sow and stack,
   – A golden sheaf might seem his brother –
To-night will ride where the angry track
   Is death and ruin in a smother,
To-night I too must face the world's mad end –
But first we'll make this day, this godlike day our friend.

Of a day in the autumn of 1917, down by Groote Vierstraat & the Swan & Edgar Corner. I was with Maycock as 'assistant' in Transport for a day or two, down towards Milky Way? [Formerly 'A Recognition'.]

[*Masks of Time*, June 1925
Undertones of War, November 1928]

La Quinque Rue

O ROAD in dizzy moonlight bleak and blue,
With forlorn effigies of farms besprawled,
With trees bitterly bare or snapped in two,
Why riddle me thus – attracted and appalled?
For surely now the grounds both left and right
Are tilled, and scarless houses undismayed
Glow in the lustrous mercy of sweet night

120

And one may hear the flute or fiddle played.
Why lead me then
Through the foul-gorged, the cemeterial fen
To fear's sharp sentries? Why do dreadful rags
Fur these bulged banks, and feebly move to the wind?
That battered drum, say why it clacks and brags?
Another and another! what's behind?
How is it that these flints flame out fire's tongue,
Shrivelling my thought? these collapsed skeletons,
What are they, and these iron hunks among?
Why clink those spades, why glare these startling suns
And topple to the wet and crawling grass,
Where the strange briars in taloned hedges twine?
What need of that stopped tread, that countersign?
O road, I know those muttering groups you pass.
I know your way of turning blood to glass.
But, I am told, to-night you safely shine
To trim roofs and cropped fields; the error's mine.

Festubert 1916-1924. It *was* a strange road to a newcomer at night in 1916.
[*Undertones of War*, November 1928]

The Ancre at Hamel: Afterwards

WHERE tongues were loud and hearts were light
    I heard the Ancre flow;
Waking oft at the mid of night
    I heard the Ancre flow.
I heard it crying, that sad rill,
    Below the painful ridge,
By the burnt unraftered mill
    And the relic of a bridge.

And could this sighing water seem
    To call me far away,
And its pale word dismiss as dream
    The voices of to-day?
The voices in the bright room chilled
    And that mourned on alone;
The silence of the full moon filled
    With that brook's troubling tone.

The struggling Ancre had no part
   In these new hours of mine,
And yet its stream ran through my heart;
   I heard it grieve and pine,
As if its rainy tortured blood
   Had swirled into my own,
When by its battered bank I stood
   And shared its wounded moan.

At Oxford? [Formerly 'The Ancre at Hamel'.]

[*New Statesman*, 12 July 1924
Masks of Time, June 1925]

"Trench Nomenclature"

GENIUS named them, as I live! What but genius could compress
In a title what man's humour said to man's supreme distress?
Jacob's Ladder ran reversed, from earth to a fiery pit extending,
With not angels but poor Angles, those for the most part descending.
Thence *Brock's Benefit* commanded endless fireworks by two nations,
Yet some voices there were raised against the rival coruscations.
Picturedome peeped out upon a dream, not Turner could surpass,
And presently the picture moved, and greyed with corpses and morass.
So down south; and if remembrance travel north, she marvels yet
At the sharp Shakespearean names, and with sad mirth her eyes are
   wet.
The Great Wall of China rose, a four-foot breastwork, fronting guns
That, when the word dropped, beat at once its silly ounces with
   brute tons;
Odd *Krab Krawl* on paper looks, and odd the foul-breathed alley
   twisted,
As one feared to twist there too, if *Minnie*, forward quean, insisted.
Where the Yser at *Dead End* floated on its bloody waters
Dead and rotten monstrous fish, note (east) *The Pike and Eel*
   headquarters.
Ah, such names and apparitions! name on name! what's in a name?
From the fabled vase the genie in his shattering horror came.

[Against line 3] Hamel.
[Against line 5] Hamel.
[Against line 7] Hamel.
[Against line 11] Hooge, Bond St., Lover's Lane, Moated Grange, Dormy House.

[Against line 13] Observatory Ridge.
These names were all real. I should like to collect more, for many were curious.
Gunner's Siding. Crow's Nest. White City. Fifth Avenue. Over the Way, Oscar's
Copse and Wild Wood.

[*Undertones of War*, November 1928]

Their Very Memory

HEAR, O hear,
They were as the welling waters,
    Sound, swift, clear,
They were all the running waters'
    Music down the greenest valley.

    Might words tell
What an echo sung within me?
    What proud bell
Clangs the last of what within me
    Pealed to be with those enlisted?

    When they smiled,
Earth's inferno changed and melted
    Greenwood mild;
Every village where they halted
    Shone with them through square and alley.

    Now my mind
Faint and few records their showings,
    Brave, strong, kind –
I'd unlock you all their doings
    But the keys are lost and twisted.

    This still grows.
Through my land be't marsh or mountain,
    Their spring flows;
But to think of them's a fountain,
    Tears of joy and music's rally.

The XIth Royal Sussex as a whole.

[*Undertones of War*, November 1928]

123

A.G.A.V.

REST you well among your race, you who cannot be dead;
Sleep lives in that country place, sleep now, pillow your head;
Time has been you could not sleep, would not if you could,
But the relief stands in the keep where you so nobly stood.

Ardour, valour, the ceaseless plan all agreed to be yours,
Wit with these familiar ran, when you went to the wars;
If one cause I have for pride, it is to have been your friend,
To have lain in shell-holes by your side, with you to have seen impend

The meteors of the hour of fire, to have talked where speech was love,
Where through fanged woods and maw-gray mire the rain and murder
    drove;
There unchanged and on your mark you laughed at some quaint clue,
And now, though time grows dull and dark, I hear, I bless you anew.

Sleep – bless you, that would not please you, gallantest dear.
Should I find you beneath yew trees? better to look for you here.
With those others whom well we knew, who went so early away,
Will you not rather gladden my view? on a dead, deathless day

Riding into the ancient town, smiling scarcely aware,
Along the dale, over the down, into the drowsy square,
There to tarry in careless ways, in church, or shop, or inn,
Leisuring after fiery days; calm-shining, more than kin;

Though dim the guns of chaos roared upon the eastern gate,
Though every hour the clock-hand scored brought closer a desperate
    date –
Well shone you then, and I would will you freedom eternal there,
Vast tumult past, and the proud sense still of vast tomorrows to dare.

Shot himself in a fit of despair, 1924, after long mental misery. A most exemplary
man in all relations.
[Against line 17] St. Omer: the Feast of Five. Described by me in a letter published
soon after (1917) in *The Blue*.
Vidler had been badly wounded, and could not endure many years after though
always full of friendship and humour.

[*Undertones of War*, November 1928]

On Reading that the Rebuilding of Ypres Approached Completion

I HEAR you now, I hear you, shy perpetual companion,
Whose deep whispers
Never wholly failed upon my twilight; but for months now
Too dimly quivered
About the crowded corridors of purpose and the clamouring
Swarmed ingresses where like squinting cobblers and half-tailors
On a weary ship that moors in dock, with grimy hatches,
Cross-purpose jangles.

Those the master, with a sudden fountain anger, towering
By his mood a Cyclops,
Back has driven, back, and snivelling, cackling, down the ladder.
I, so springing,
Have lashed the buzzing bullies out, and in the freed air pause now,
Hearing you, whose face is ever one and ever million,
This dear dead one's, this dear living one's, no man's and all men's,
True map of Flanders.

Wordless language! well to me this moment making music,
Utmost union.
So, so, so we meet again; here we know our coexistence,
And your voice is
My self-utterance, while the region thus is hush and lonely,
Not a charlatan thought there left to gnaw my heart is skulking,
Nor one sunbeam sets the tingling atoms dancing by me
Like doubt's mad apings.

But my danger lies even here, even now worn weak and nerveless
I go drooping,
Heavy-headed, and would sleep thus lulled with your love's fulness.
Sharply awake me
With fierce words, cold as the fangs of bayonets in the frozen saps,
Simple as the fact that you must kill, or go for rations,
As clear as morning blue, as red and grotesque as the open mouths
Of winter corpses.

I hear you now: the voice, the voice of marching bowed battalions,
Of one strong soldier,
Now black-haired Daniells, now more saxon Clifford, now hale
  Worley –
O, speak. Our old tongue.
"I was Thy neighbour once, thou rugged Pile, thou whiteness, Ypres,
How mighty in thy misery, how royal in thy ravishing,
With fingers brittle as ice, I champed and clattered by the convent
And shouted orders;

Which echoes scrambling on the snowy walls and eyeless bulwarks
Made haste to carry,
But they could not, for the curious air was overburdened
With ancient echoes.
Vaults below the convent, when they pitied and would shelter,
Scarce could lure me, counter-lured though eyelids pressed like roof-
  leads;
Nor such sights as the circling pigeons of poor St. Martin held me
From my huge labours.

Blood-like swam the moon, the city's sable wounds lurked,
Still she cried out,
Be most constant! Thence with clumsy zeal and sacred cursing
Through the shrill grass,
Through the trapping thicket-thorns of death, that sudden planter,
While in the light of the moon and snow his blueness masked all
  faces,
Stern I went, the weaker kind most mercilessly heartening
To the shambles

All for her, that gap-toothed witch, that beauty at the butcher's,
To me intrusted;
Nor did I desert her, though without so much as a second's warning,
Some harsh slash-hook
Slit my skull and poured out all the fountains of my senses;
Burst the bloodgates; still I came, and went and came to man her,
Left Posthoornstraat and Goldfish Château, joined with waxen
  hands the cleft trench,
Hating and loving.

She, with that, was sometime mild and from the spectre ruin
Herself seemed lifting;
Walking in some silent moments, to the glimmer of candles,
I smiled and marvelled
How the dusky houses in the rainy gloom with feigned renaissance

126

Stood for life, and surely from the opened doors would be duly coming
Women and lightfoot children, lover there in the lamplight grow to
    lover –
Death, stop that laughing!

Nor has ever been the man, not Milton with his angels,
Who found such chorus,
Such diapason and amazement in strange old oriental
Fantasy-places,
As I in gross and clod-like names of hamlets by the city;
The fame of Kemmel clanged, and Athens dulled: I listened
If one spoke of Zonnebeke with thronged imagination,
A dazing distance.

For words spoke at the *Mermaid*, I would not give the meanest
That I heard echoing
In some green-shuttered *Nachtegaal or Kasteel*, a brief evening,
While the panes were jumping;
Far less one of the sweet astounding jests and sallies
That dared contest with smoking salvoes the forlorn hope's attention,
That wreathed the burning steel that slew with man's eternal laurel
In that one city.

For her was much accomplished, and she will not forget me,
Whose name is Legion;
She will know who knew her best, and with his rough warm garment
Would have wrapt her;
Her midnight tears will ever well as grayly she remembers
The hillock's signifying tree, that choked and gouged and miry
Was like a cross, but such a cross that there no bleeding Figure
Might hang without tautology.

And mine she is; they now may build, sign and assign there,
Above bright doorways
Paint in gold their titles; shrine among their tufted gardens,
As did their elders,
The statues of their mild desire Arcadian: but I
Am in the soil and sap, and in the becks and conduits
My blood is flowing, and my sigh of consummation
Is the wind in the rampart trees."

In Japan.

[*Undertones of War*, November 1928]

Another Journey from Bethune to Cuinchy

I SEE you walking
To a pale petalled sky,
And the green silent water
Is resting there by;
It seems like bold madness
But that "you" is I.

I long to interpret
That voice of a bell
So silver and simple,
Like a wood-dove-egg shell,
On the bank where you are walking –
It was I heard it well.

At the lock the sky bubbles
Are dancing and dying,
Some the smallest of pearls,
Some moons, and all flying,
Returning, and melting –
You watched them, half-crying.

This is Marie-Louise,
You need not have told me –
I remember her eyes
And the Cognac she sold me –
It is you that are sipping it;
Even so she cajoled me.

Her roof and her windows
Were nothing too sound,
And here and there holes
Some forty feet round
(Antiquer than Homer)
Encipher the ground.

Do you jib at my tenses?
Who's who? you or I?
Do you own Bethune

128

And that grave eastward sky?
Bethune is miles off now,
'Ware wire and don't die.

The telegraph posts
Have revolted at last,
And old Perpendicular
Leans to the blast,
The rigging hangs ragging
From each plunging mast.

What else would you fancy,
For here it is war?
My thanks, you young upstart,
I've been here before –
I know this Division,
And hate this damned Corps.

"Kingsclere" hath its flowers,
And piano to boot;
The coolest of cellars, –
– Your finest salute!
You fraudulent wretch –
You appalling recruit!

O haste, for the darnel
Hangs over the trench,
As yellow as the powder
Which kills with a stench!
Shall you go or I go?
O I'll go – don't mench!

But both of us slither
Between the mossed banks,
And through thirsty chalk
Where the red-hatted cranks
Have fixed a portcullis
With notice-board – thanks!

A mad world, my masters!
Whose masters? my lad,
If you are not I,
It is I who am mad;
Let's report to the company,
Your mess, egad.

Well, now sir (though lime juice
Is nothing to aid),
This young fellow met me,
And kindly essayed
To guide me – but now it seems
I am betrayed.

He says he is I,
And that I am not he;
But the same omened sky
Led us both, we agree, –
If we cannot commingle,
Pray take him and me.

For where the numb listener
Lies in the dagged weed,
I'll see your word law,
And this youth has agreed
To let me use *his* name –
Take the will for the deed.

And what if the whistle
Of the far-away train
Come moan-like through mist
Over Coldstream Lane,
Come mocking old love
Into waking again?

And the thinkings of life,
Whether those of your blood,
Or the manifold soul
Of field and of flood –
What if they come to you
Bombed in the mud?

Well, now as afore
I should wince so, no doubt,
And still to my star
I should cling, all about,
And muddy one midnight
We all will march out.

– Sir, this man may talk,
But he surely omits
That a crump any moment

May blow us to bits;
On this rock his identity –
Argument splits.

I see him walking
In a golden-green ground,
Where pinafored babies
And skylarks abound,
But that's his own business.
My time for trench round.

Imaginary dialogue between E.B. 1916 & E.B. 1924 or later.

[*Undertones of War*, November 1928]

Flanders Now

THERE, where before no master action struck
The grim Fate in the face, and cried "What now?",
Where gain and commonplace lay in their ruck,
And pulled the beetroots, milked the muddy cow,
Heard the world's rumours, wished themselves good luck,
And slept, and rose, and lived and died somehow, –

A light is striking keen as angels' spears,
Brightness outwelling, cool as roses, there;
From every crossroad majesty appears,
Each cottage gleams like Athens on the air;
Ghosts by broad daylight, answered not by fears
But bliss unwordable, are walking there.

Who thirsts, or aches, or gropes as going blind?
Friend, drink with me at these fair-foliaged wells,
Or on the bruised life lay this unction kind,
Or mark this light that lives in lily-bells,
There rests and always shall the wandering mind,
Those clumsy farms to-day grow miracles:

Since past each wall and every common mark,
Field path and wooden bridge, there once went by
The flower of manhood, daring the huge dark,
The famished cold, the roaring in the sky;

131

They died in splendour, these who claimed no spark
Of glory save the light in a friend's eye.

[Formerly 'Old Battlefields'.]

[*Harper's Monthly Magazine*, Vol. 154, March 1927
Undertones of War, November 1928]

The Watchers

I HEARD the challenge "Who goes there?"
Close-kept but mine through midnight air;
I answered and was recognised
And passed, and kindly thus advised:
"There's someone crawlin' through the grass
By the red ruin, or there was,
And them machine guns been a firin'
All the time the chaps was wirin',
So sir if you're goin' out
You'll keep your 'ead well down no doubt."

When will the stern fine "Who goes there?"
Meet me again in midnight air?
And the gruff sentry's kindness, when
Will kindness have such power again?
It seems, as now I wake and brood,
And know my hour's decrepitude,
That on some dewy parapet
The sentry's spirit gazes yet,
Who will not speak with altered tone
When I at last am seen and known.

[*St. Martin's Review*, No. 441, November 1927
Undertones of War, November 1928]

An Infantryman

PAINFULLY writhed the few last weeds upon those houseless uplands,
   Cleft pods had dropt their blackened seeds into the trampled clay,
Wind and rain were running loose, and icy flew the whiplash;
   Masked guns like autumn thunder drummed the outcast year away.

Hidden a hundred yards ahead with winter's blinding passion,
   The mule-beat track appeared half dead, even war's hot blood congealed;
The half-dug trenches brimmed like troughs, the camps lay slushed and
      empty,
   Unless those bitter whistlings proved Death's army in the field.

Over the captured ridge above the hurt battalion waited,
   And hardly had sense left to prove if ghost or living passed
From hole to hole with sunken eyes and slow ironic orders,
   While fiery fountains burst and clanged – and there your lot was cast.

Yet I saw your health and youth go brightening to the vortex,
   The ghosts on guard, the storm uncouth were then no match for you;
You smiled, you sang, your courage rang, and to this day I hear it,
   Sunny as a May-day dance, along that spectral avenue.

Having nothing much to do one afternoon near Mailly (I think) James Cassels and
I went for a long walk in the rain. The poem is on him. 1916.

[*English Review*, Vol. 46, May 1928
Retreat, May 1928 (revised)]

Inaccessibility in the Battlefield

FORGOTTEN streams, yet wishful to be known,
      With humble moan
In rushy channels working, called us on;
   These might have with as good result
      Remained occult
      And gray and dumb;
   For where they curled and called we could not come.

Some tottering hut they called the Moated Grange
    Bade our steps range
And cramped routine for rural loves exchange;
   That thatched spectre might as well
     With some fierce shell
     Have sunk to earth;
A jealous god declined our going forth.

And that delightful maybush, that above
    The dead mill-drove
With rose-lipped courtesy and whispering love
   Enchanted, was not ours to touch.
     Between, this grutch,
     This staring curse
Made a blind wall, and kept our lips averse.

The simple road proposed most kind desires
    For further spires,
Hearths, garden-grots, dove-cots; but fang-fixed wires
   And ambushed airy murder lay
     All day, that way;
     A simple road, –
The rampart where the sleepless phantom strode.

[*Fortnightly Review*, N.S. Vol. 126, 2 September 1929
Near and Far, September 1929]

War's People

THROUGH the tender amaranthine domes
Of angel-evenings echoing summer song,
  Through the black rock-tombs
Of winter, and where autumn floods prolong
  The midnight roar and tumbling thunder,
  Through spring's daisy-peeping wonder,
Round and beyond and over and under,
    I see our homes.

Bloom, healing rosiness and wild-wine flowers,
Or lift a vain wing in the mire, dropt leaf;
Storm-spirit, coil your lightnings round mad towers;
Go forth, you marching Seasons, horsemen Hours;
Blow silver triumphs, Joy, and knell, grey Grief.

These after-pieces will not now dispel
The scene and action that was learned in hell.
These charming veils a thought has strength to waft
With one quick thrill aloft; and then we view
    Seasons and hours we better knew,
Desperate budding of untimely green,
Skies and soft cloud-land savagely serene,
Steel or mere sleet that beat past-caring bones,
Night-tempest not so loud as those long moans
From low-gorged lairs, which outshine Zion's towers,
Weak rags of walls, the forts of godlike powers.
    We went, returned,
But came with that far country learned;
Strange stars, and dream-like sounds, changed speech and
      law are ours.

Written a time after 1918, so I think the 'estrangement' was deep.

[*Near and Far*, September 1929]

Return of the Native

ABOUT the Ramparts, quiet as a mother
Kissing a child in dreams, the summer night
Cast a soft veil; the power beyond the stars
Was now intent upon the consonance
Of boughs and airs and earthy purities.

We stood, hard-watching in the eastward dark
A glowing pyre and vapour by Hill Sixty,
And wondered who was mocking, Peace or War?
The last train answered with far-dying echoes,
And passed along the cutting; now the plain
Lay in its first sleep, all its dwellings slept
And called the night their own. The old law here
Had come again with peasant tread to claim
So full and unabated property
That not one mark of a mad occupation
Might be conceived.

          We only, watching, seemed
The battlefield, if we were not deluded
By dreaming ecstasies; could we have seen

The ordinance of eternity reversed,
And night disdained and dazzled into day,
And day shot into gulfs of glaring gloom?
Man in our time, and with our help, grew here
A pale Familiar; here he struck the Sun,
And for a season turned the Sun to blood;
Many such nights as this his Witch and he
Unmasked their metal, and with poisonous work
Broke the fair sanctuary of this world's rest
And circumvented God. But now misrule
With all its burning rout had gone on the wind,
Leaving us with the south-west breeze to whisper
In bushes younger than the brows it cooled,
Foreheads entrenched with all the argument
Of what was once Time's vast compulsion, now
Incapable to stir a weed or moth.

                                        Ypres, 1929

[*St. Martin's Review*, No. 465, June 1929
Undertones of War, June 1930 (second edition)]

EXPERIENCE AND SOLILOQUY

Unteachable

To some, thoughts flying into futurity's cloud;
To some, pale provings mocking time and space;
To some, the puzzling out to-day's hoarse crowd;
To each his own: I run a backward race.

I have been wandering distant roads, have striven
To win new comprehensions; much in vain.
There's that within me cares not what is given
By such migrations; of a stubborn grain,

This Hodge-like serf and tyrant trudges on,
Grudges and growls at all my innovations,
Lets new things go to rack when I am gone
On other errands, sticks to's old vocations.

Caelum, non animum – nay, scarce he'll see
An altered sky, and this, all said and done,
I like him for; he'll sit by his old tree,
To eat his bit of dinner, out of the sun.

In Japan.

[Nation & Athenaeum, 11 October 1924
English Poems, January 1926]

The Crown Inn

Round all its nooks and corners goes
    The evening talk, in this old inn;
The darkening room by use well knows
    Each thread of life that these upspin.

The triumphs of the wooer, player,
    Eclogues of praise for mead and beer,
The fabled wealth, the generous fair
    Ring round the wonted changes here.

In elmtrees' gloom the western ray
    Drowns, the sad cloud steals like a shroud
Drawn over one that died to-day,
    And to my spirit memory-bowed

The world with all its wars and wails
    Seems turning slow; but here are some
With whom no black gazette prevails,
    Whom no disaster renders dumb.

Against the thunderclouds of race
    Their cottage candles give them light,
They like their clocks keep one same pace
    While empires shudder into night.

Denardiston? [Formerly 'The Crown'.]
[*Masks of Time*, June 1925]

The Midnight Skaters

THE hop-poles stand in cones,
    The icy pond lurks under,
The pole-tops steeple to the thrones
    Of stars, sound gulfs of wonder;
But not the tallest there, 'tis said,
Could fathom to this pond's black bed.

Then is not death at watch
    Within those secret waters?
What wants he but to catch
    Earth's heedless sons and daughters?
With but a crystal parapet
Between, he has his engines set.

Then on, blood shouts, on, on,
    Twirl, wheel and whip above him,
Dance on this ball-floor thin and wan,

Use him as though you love him;
Court him, elude him, reel and pass,
And let him hate you through the glass.

Back to Congelow.

[*Masks of Time*, June 1925]

Old Pleasures Deserted

COBWEBS and kisks have crept
    On what so smiled, so shone, so smiled;
Fen-gotten fogs have wept,
Rust and moth have ate and slept,
    Foul-coiling growths defiled.

Morn's golden sandals lie
    Slouched and unnoted; moiled in weed,
Diana's silver archery
    Sails no shrill wind; Pan's maiden-reed
Is sunk to atoms grey and dry;
Those flowers that lost Persephone
    Left in the sun, are shrunk to screed.

There were stones and shells
    That a god brought me from a brook,
They gleamed as miracles,
    They're now – I dare not look.
By a clear green pool a kingfisher flew,
    Left with me an angel's plume;
Where greybirds sang cool orchards through
    I found a flute that put forth bloom.

Michael's plume, flowery flute
    Were here, and thousand beauties more;
Beneath this shroud of disrepute,
    These scurfs and soilings, lay rich store:
But creeping on, the shade of death
    Has changed this air;
Gaspingly I take my breath.
    Yet did you dare,
Through this hushed and kisky den
    Find them you might,

139

And touch them into truth again
May-morning bright.

[*English Poems*, January 1926]

Rue du Bois

HARMONIOUS trees, whose lit and lissom graces
　　For ever brighten on my hastening eye,
Calmed by whose leisure, by whose great griefs raptured,
　　I cared not if the word were live or die,

Oh that I might with kisses and caresses
　　Reveal that love to you, most lovely Powers,
And like the sun or trembling dew be welcome,
　　And see no winter to our green amours!

This heart that glows at myriad-mantled beauty
　　And at a gleam in voice or touch or eye
Is lost and lispering, dazzled and disastered,
　　This heart the plaything of the Passing By –

O could it but be held by these wood-wonders,
　　That time but gently, gently shine and sing!
Death first! and even in death this heart, dust-crumbled,
　　Will never give an aspen to the spring.

I remember the big trees between Béthune and Bois de Biez in the summer of 1916.

[*English Poems*, January 1926]

Warning to Troops

WHAT soldier guessed that where the stream descended
In country dance beneath the colonnade
Of elms which cooled the halted troop, it played
Sly music, barely noted, never ended?
Or who, from war's concerns a moment missed,
At some church door turned white as came to him

One gold note struck by the hidden organist,
One note long-drawn through caverns cool and dim?

O marcher, hear. But when thy route and tramp
Pause by some falling stream, or holy door,
Be the deaf adder; bear not back to camp
That embryo music. Double not thy war.
Shun all such sweet prelusion. March, sing, roar,
Lest perilous silence gnaw thee evermore.

I was haunted by a music from the church door at Bethune.

[*English Poems*, January 1926]

The Complaint

THE village spoke: "You come again,
You left me for a world of men.
   Tell,
How you feel now my former spell?"

And I: "Sweet simpleton, old home –
Much charged, with puzzled heart I come;
   Still,
I think you are the nonpareil."

At that a breeze, a sigh was heard,
And thus the traveller caught the word,
   "Child,
Love's just and gentle; love you smiled;

But was it not my creed and dream
To fit you for a mightier theme?
   Proud
You stepped away to join the crowd.

And since, what hills, what skies you've known,
What streets of strength, what speaking stone!
   More,
The drama of terrestrial war;

And love the Atlantis, far and near,
And genius brightening sphere on sphere,

141

Bounds
That only seemed thought's pleasure-grounds.

Thence come you with this accent dim,
With eyes that gaze till the tears brim?
   I
But look, how small and poor I lie."

The sunny grass danced on the wall,
The smithy clanged, old Jesse Hall
   Flung
His jacket off, and scythed and sung;

From school the hungry youngsters rushed,
The caravan passed, the mill sluice gushed.
   "Dear,"
I answered, "all my ways led here."

[*London Mercury*, Vol. 14, No. 80, June 1926
Retreat, May 1928 (revised)]

On the Portrait of a Colonel G.H.H.

WHEN now at this stern depth and shade of soul
I lift my eyes to that most honoured face,
And yearn towards that harmony and whole
Of soldier creed and act and pride of place,
The eye's shrewd humour, the lip's generous grace,
The stirring zest, the power to make and give,
I feel my youth awake afresh and live,
And bugled morning glows and climbs apace.

Some stubborn clouds of conscience stain that prime,
And chilly creeps the muttering breeze, regret;
But still this picture kindles coming time,
And bids me gird myself for crossroads yet
Where through the inhuman tempestings of night
This man's commanding trust will be my sight.

It has been so always, even if we have not been called on to prove it in later action.
[Formerly 'Portrait of a Colonel'.]

[*London Mercury*, Vol. 18, No. 103, May 1928
Retreat, May 1928 (revised)]

Report on Experience

I HAVE been young, and now am not too old;
And I have seen the righteous forsaken,
His health, his honour and his quality taken.
    This is not what we were formerly told.

I have seen a green country, useful to the race,
Knocked silly with guns and mines, its villages vanished,
Even the last rat and last kestrel banished –
    God bless us all, this was peculiar grace.

I knew Seraphina; Nature gave her hue,
Glance, sympathy, note, like one from Eden.
I saw her smile warp, heard her lyric deaden;
    She turned to harlotry; – this I took to be new.

Say what you will, our God sees how they run.
These disillusions are His curious proving
That He loves humanity and will go on loving;
    Over there are faith, life, virtue in the sun.

'Unpremeditated', & almost thrown away.

[*Near and Far*, September 1929]

The Study

WHILE I sit penning plans of dead affairs,
And hardly pause but when some wilder gust
Drives the mist shower with a more savage thrust
Against my window, hark! what sweeter cares
Find a shy voice, that makes my writing cease,
And in this room of shelves, and books, and files,
The ranked and crested past, what pleasure smiles!

The dead withdraw, the living share their peace.
For down my chimney with the dripping rain
Come tiny trills and chirps and silvery notes
Like whistling mice; it's nesting-time again;
There in the dimness gape what eager throats
Of the new brood, who through this tempest dun
Know they are for the singing and the sun!

[*Near and Far*, September 1929]

Values

TILL darkness lays a hand on these gray eyes
And out of man my ghost is sent alone,
It is my chance to know that force and size
Are nothing but by answered undertone.
No beauty even of absolute perfection
Dominates here – the glance, the pause, the guess
Must be my amulets of resurrection;
Raindrops may murder, lightnings may caress.

There I was tortured, but I cannot grieve;
There crowned and palaced – visibles deceive.
That storm of belfried cities in my mind
Leaves me my vespers cool and eglantined.
From love's wide-flowering mountain-side I chose
This sprig of green, in which an angel shows.

[*The Observer*, 2 June 1929]

In Wiltshire

(Suggested by points of similarity with the Somme country.)

FAIREST of valleys, in this full-bloomed night,
  Whose air so lullingly,
  Whose dusk so understandingly
Embraces us, and gives us more than light,

O happy valley, with your poplars manned
  Beneath the visiting moon,

144

And talking to the loitering moon,
Vast as desire, and by an owl-call spanned,

Perfection is your name; yet (foolish prayer!)
    Well would it be for some,
    And safer your dim grace for some,
If nothing in your presence could compare

With a far place. That shuttered lampless mill,
    Those white-glanced pools are like,
    These tangled cliffs are all too like
A valley where our dream-selves tremble still.

The wires and poles that cut the ridge and sky,
    The blackness of these groves,
    The secret paths of river-groves,
These fits and starts of sound, identify.

My feet, along this road, above that stream,
    Drop into marching-time,
    Make wild arithmetic of time –
So like this valley and that dead one seem.

Resemble less, warm vale! that vale of tears;
    Some signs and shades forego.
    Cause not our very joy to go
Among old valley-tombs of flesh and blood and years.

Staying at Wilsford.

[*The Observer*, 15 September 1929
Poems 1914-30, December 1930]

Chances of Remembrance

I

"TURN not from me;
I am the last rainbow that you may ever see.
    Take the rich surprise
    Of the skies
    With all your eyes;
Dream from what labyrinths of bloom my wings arise. –

145

　　　See,
Even a rainbow dies."

II

"You see me here,
　And you huddle past and shiver;
　　One glance, you disappear,
Leaving me, a dull brown thicket, beside a gray-gorged river.
　　I beg no grace of yours;
You have seen me, I go with you, in or out of doors;
　　My thin blood will not wash out,
　　My purple brambles will mantle you about,
　　My thorny claspings pierce
　　Into your verse."

[*The Observer*, 2 February 1930
Poems 1914-30, December 1930]

The Sunlit Vale

I SAW the sunlit vale, and the pastoral fairy-tale;
The sweet and bitter scent of the may drifted by;
And never have I seen such a bright bewildering green,
　　But it looked like a lie,
　　Like a kindly meant lie.

When gods are in dispute, one a Sidney, one a brute,
It would seem that human sense might not know, might not spy;
But though nature smile and feign where foul play has stabbed and
　　slain,
　　There's a witness, an eye,
　　Nor will charms blind that eye.

Nymph of the upland song and the sparkling leafage young,
For your merciful desire with these charms to beguile,
For ever be adored; muses yield you rich reward;
　　But you fail, though you smile –
　　That other does not smile.

[Formerly 'The Failure'.]

[*London Mercury*, Vol. 20, No. 120, October 1929
Poems 1914-30, December 1930]

CAN YOU REMEMBER?

Winter Stars

FIERCE in flaming millions, ready to strike they stood,
The stars of unknown will, above our field and wood;
You who have seen the midnight preparing a dawn of war
May raise imagination to see them ready to roar
Their sparkling death-way down; and while they waited the order
Some came flying from nowhere, and launched what
   looked like murder,
Rushing beyond our border, and detonating too far
For us to hear. No need to hear. Watching each angry star
I thought our thicket lifted its stack of bayonets
Stiffly against the overthrow of Nature's parapets;
And marching amain from the highlands came our stream
   to see this through;
Deep and hoarse and gathering force, it swore to die or do;
Under the intelligence of strange foes, it sang to self and chance,
Answering all that wildfire with the gleam of its foaming advance.

[*The Observer*, 4 January 1931
To Themis, December 1931]

Fancy and Memory

ADIEU, young Fancy with the gipsy eye,
Sly slip of a ghost, your time with me is done;
Once we were bold together, now good-bye,
Once you lit heaven, I now prefer the sun:
Flit on, delicious false one, and still please
The hearts you may awhile; bring Sullen to his knees.

147

Your sister Memory is more welcome now.
She if she feigns at all seems without guile;
She tells no tale for time to disavow,
No contraries but she will reconcile;
With her I wonder less than love, and calm
Comes with no greater stir than dewy nightflowers' balm.

She makes the tiny nautilus sail sweet
Upon the shell-smooth lulling ocean-stream;
And men who died arise and smile to see't,
And I am free to talk of life with them;
She gives me temple-steps in warm west rain,
The crystal summit, thunderous pinewood, ripening plain.

Music she has that richly speaks her mind;
So singing, she with Orpheus vies; I hear,
And Flemish church-tower vanes glint in the wind
And man and horse and crow again live near, –
Man, horse, and guns and mines and tanks renew
Daybreak's demented duel – Memory, *et tu?*

[*The Observer*, 27 December 1931
Halfway House, November 1932]

Mental Hospital

I: TWO IN A CORNER

TRANQUIL enough they sit apart
        In this safe tomb;
    Their eyes on one another turned
    Reveal the one thing they have learned,
In life, if that word fit their gloom:
        Heart given to heart.

If beauty be no myth or mode
        Conventional,
    These sister-faces are the least
    With lineament of beauty blest;
And yet I would not say they showed
        No grace at all.

CAN YOU REMEMBER?

Hardly aware of joy or grief
    As two extremes,
  They sit half-lurking, leaning nearer,
  Touching cheeks, true touch, no error;
One bright fact still flowering belief
    Amid dull dreams.

II: POOR TOM'S WELCOME

ALONG the rows the party goes,
    Along the rows of withered men,
The girls with perfumed flower-like clothes,
    The youths whose strength's the strength of ten –
      And humbly sit those withered men,
      The slow ones, in their den.

They see the raree-show float by,
    They eye it with no wild concern –
It will go by; it's bright enough,
But there's no seizing such cloud-stuff.
      One roars his sudden loud return
      To old ways, then stops stern.

But one there is who cannot stay,
    Unmoved; the dwarf, he leaves his chair,
And shuffling works his apeish way
    To the strangers; and with smiling air
      And no word said, holds out his hand,
      And looks his *you will understand.*

They take his hand, now that, now this,
    And he smiles on; and then they're past.
Done is the courtesy, cold the bliss.
    He sinks away as a dead leaf cast
      Into some slack gray pool; the light,
      Was brief, how long the night!

[*Halfway House*, November 1932]

149

The Memorial, 1914-1918

AGAINST this lantern, shrill, alone
The wind springs out of the plain.
Such winds as this must fly and moan
Round the summit of every stone
On every hill; and yet a strain
Beyond the measure elsewhere known
Seems here.
        Who cries? who mingles with the gale?
Whose touch, so anxious and so weak, invents
A coldness in the coldness? in this veil
Of whirling mist what hue of clay consents?
Can atoms intercede?

And are those shafted bold constructions there,
Mines more than golden, wheels that outrace need,
Crowded corons, victorious chimneys – are
Those touched with question too? pale with the dream
Of those who in this aether-stream
Are urging yet their painful, woundful theme?

Day flutters as a curtain, stirred
By a hidden hand; the eye grows blurred.
Those towers, uncrystalled, fade.
The wind from north and east and south
Comes with its starved white mouth
And at this crowning trophy cannot rest –
No, speaks as something past plain words distressed.

Be still, if these your voices are; this monolith
For you and your high sleep was made.
Some have had less.
No gratitude in deathlessness?
No comprehension of the tribute paid?

You would speak still? Who with?

[*Halfway House*, November 1932]

Inscribed in War Books

I

MORE rarely now the echo of these men
Sounds through the years;
In towns which knew their rifle-numbers then
Not smiles nor tears
Start at their memory; and this might be well,
Did such oblivion tell
Of an unwarlike and regenerate age,
And not of battles dark and worse presage.

II

These marched towards Death, or what seemed he,
And still their sense was liberty;
As though his bulk and bulwark meant
Not close but opening of event,
As though his wall would prove an arch
And only dignify their march,
And, that got by, the curving road
Led where new airs and waters flowed,
New stars, new flowers, new faces shone;
Whatever here had lost some tone
With all its song should be restored
To their own heightened souls' accord.

[*Halfway House*, November 1932]

November 1, 1931

WE talked of ghosts; and I was still alive;
And I that very day was thirty-five;
Alone once more, I stared about my room
And wished some ghost would be a friend and come;
I cared not of what shape or semblance; terror
Was nothing in comparison with error;
I wished some ghost would come, to talk of fate,

And tell me why I drove my pen so late,
And help with observations on my knack
Of being always on the bivouac,
Here and elsewhere, for ever changing ground,
Finding and straightway losing what I found,
Baffled in time, fumbling each sequent date,
Mistaking Magdalen for the Menin Gate.
This much I saw without transmortal talk,
That war had quite changed my sublunar walk –
Forgive me, dear, honoured and saintly friends
Ingratitude suspect not; this transcends.
Forgive, O sweet red-smiling love, forgive,
If this is life, for your delight I live;
How every lamp, how every pavement flames
Your beauty at me, and your faith acclaims!
But from my silences your kindness grew,
And I surrendered for the time to you,
And still I hold you glorious and my own,
I'd take your hands, your lips; but I'm alone.
So I was forced elsewhere, and would accost
For colloquy and guidance some kind ghost.
As one that with a serious trust was sent
Afar, and bandits seized him while he went,
And long delayed, so I; I yearned to catch
What I should know before my grave dispatch
Was to be laid before that General
Who in a new Time cries 'backs to the wall.'
No ghost was granted me; and I must face
Uncoached the masters of that Time and Space,
And there with downcast murmurings set out
What my gross late appearance was about.

[*Halfway House*, November 1932]

Unlucky Allusions

'WHEN I was here in the War,' he said,
    'There was life enough in the place;
'There was always a crowd at the Golden Head
    And' – . The lady made a face,
And (wrapping the bottle) reproved him: 'Ah;
    'On n'était pas très correct, là-bas.'

One day he'll make his mistake again,
    When he's having a word at the Gate;
'Yes, we saw some great nights, and some very good men
    At the Cock' – . 'You needn't wait,'
St. Peter will hastily interject,
    'Là-bas, on n'était pas très correct.'

[*Choice or Chance*, November 1934]

The Branch Line

PROFESSING loud energy, out of the junction departed
The branch-line engine. The small train rounded the bend
Watched by us pilgrims of summer, and most by me, –
Who had known this picture since first my travelling started,
And knew it as sadly pleasant, the usual end
Of singing returns to beloved simplicity.

The small train went from view behind the plantation,
Monotonous, – but there's a grace in monotony!
I felt its journey, I watched in imagination
Its brown smoke spun with sunshine wandering free
Past the great weir with its round flood-mirror beneath,
And where the magpie rises from orchard shadows,
And among the oasts, and like a rosy wreath
Mimicking children's flower-play in the meadows.

The thing so easy, so daily, of so small stature
Gave me another picture: of war's warped face
Where still the sun and the leaf and the lark praised Nature,
But no little engine bustled from place to place;
When summer succeeded summer, yet only ghosts
Or to-morrow's ghosts could venture hand or foot
In the track between the terrible telegraph-posts,–
The end of all things lying between the hut
Which lurked this side, and the shattered local train
That.
    So easy it was; and should that come again – .

[*The Spectator*, 23 June 1933
Choice or Chance, November 1934]

153

Some Talk of Peace –

DARK War, exploding loud mephitic mines,
Or with a single shot destroying twenty,
Was in a way reserved, polite and dainty.
Then there was not much felt of cold designs,
Murder that chanced seemed past man's guiding-lines,
And conscience never flushed for that grim throe.

Peace, lovely lady, is too fine to shout
Her power abroad; seldom she lays us low
As the machine-guns stretched the storm-troops out;
She gives us time to answer Yes or No.
She may not kill; she even keeps alive
Those whom their faces or their foes deprive
Of joy and equity; and we live in doubt
Whether her sins or War's more misery sow.

[*Choice or Chance*, November 1934]

The Lost Battalion

'TO dream again.' That chance. There were no fences,
No failures, no impossibles, no tenses.
Here's the huge sulky ship, the captain's room,
The swilling decks like hillsides, the iron boom
Of ocean's pugilism, black faces, low
Corner-cabals – 'Where are we bound? d'ye know?'
And now, long months being drummed into our lives,
The bells ring back and fro, the boat arrives –
We've seen this place, does no one know its *name*?
Name missing. But we'll get there all the same.
It's all the same. I thought the war was done.
We'll have to hurry, the Battalion's gone.
How on again? Only an Armistice.
I thought my nerves weren't quite so bad as this.
That white house hangs on strangely, turn sharp right,
And the instant war spreads gray and mute in sight.
I feel my old gear on my back, and know

154

My general job in this forthcoming show;
But what's the catch, the difference? Someone speak!
Name wanted, or I shan't get there this week.

[*Choice or Chance*, November 1934]

From Age to Age

RETARDED into history's marble eyes
Is their quick challenge and ability;
All the expression of their enterprise,
The fierce, the rapt, the generous and the free.
Behold their monument; no more is now to see.

Travel this cool white day across this plain,
Count farms and haycocks, think of dead event,
Count all these graves, count every pang and pain
Which put them here; but life will not relent.
Hardly the deathmask held one hour their last intent.

Action, eternal fire! from brain to brain,
From race to race, and age to age on-leaping,
Leaves the charred embers to the steady rain;
Over the skeleton the grass comes creeping,
And life's too short for wondering, too aflame for weeping.

[Formerly 'The Only Answer'.]

[*The Spectator*, 17 March 1933
Choice or Chance, November 1934]

To The Southdowns

On their dining again together, 1934

COME, and defy or else forget
The hurrying years; we're Southdowns yet,
And if we heard the bugle-call,
Could still fall in and beat them all –
But peaceful now the call arrives;
No arms to slope but forks and knives,

155

No sandbags here though we may be
Windbags for once and still agree;
We here may sit around and dine
Unvexed by gas alarm or mine,
And know the rations will come up
Without objections from Von Krupp.
In Pop. we banqueted no doubt
On *vin-blong*, malaga-and-stout,
On 'eggs and ships'; with Ruby Queens
We once crowned feeds of pork and beans.
Some happy days there were. But some –
However, that's all over. Come;
The M.M.P.'s have lost their way,
And no day now will be Z Day.
No foot, no kit inspection; nor
Must we by eyewash win the war;
The duckboard-track is all deserted,
The very Padre's been converted,
The General's raising veal and swedes,–
Those new recruits the Empire needs, –
The Transport now could hardly tell
A mule from a monkey; all is well!
The old cross-roads are calm to-night,
Jerry's relieving, stars shine bright –
So, to All Ranks good appetite!

[*Southdown Battalions' Association Annual Dinner*, 24 March 1934
Choice or Chance, November 1934 (revised)]

At Rugmer

AMONG sequestered farms and where brown orchards
Weave in the thin and coiling wind, and where
The pale cold river ripples still as moorhens
Work their restless crossing,
Among such places, when October warnings
Sound from each kex and thorn and shifting leaf,
We well might wander, and renew some stories
Of a dim time when we were kex and thorn,
Sere leaf, ready to hear a hissing wind
Whip down and wipe us out; our season seemed
At any second closing.

156

So, we were wrong. But we have lived this landscape,
And have an understanding with these shades.

[*Choice or Chance*, November 1934]

War Cemetery

WHY are they dead? Is Adam's seed so strong
That these bold lives cut down mean nothing lost?
Indeed, they would have died; ourselves ere long
Will take our turn. That cheque is signed and crossed.
But, though this dying business still concerns
The lot of us, there seems something amiss
When twenty million sudden funeral urns
Are called for. Have you no hypothesis?
Was heaven prepared for this abrupt incursion,
Was the word out to modernize the choir?
Or had the other congress (no aspersion)
A labour problem and a dwindling fire?
    In any case they're dead, and by their dates
    Nine-tenths should now be laughing with their mates.

No one can say they are not buried well,
At least as much of them as could be found;
Here grow abundant herbs of sweetest smell
And the rose here beats all; the easy sound
Of shears or scythe comes from the grassy border,
The blackbird runs across the shaven green.
Dressed by the right, fallen in with perfect order,
The dead contingents in gray stone are seen.
Some races cling to something more than stone;
'See, this was Georges, in his new uniform,
Bright cheeks, straight eyes – you really should have known
Our Georges.' The photograph through sun and storm
    Lives its short life, says something that Georges said,
    But one still wonders why he should be dead.

Man, like some friends of his, is a grand fellow
For generous leaps into appalling holes;
Among his fears, the fear of seeming yellow
Urges him far, displaces, uncontrols.
Then he is prone to vanity, will dance

157

On steeple-points so he may end notorious,
And from his flowerful work will follow chance
Into the cannon's mouth to be called glorious.
But Georges arriving at the barracks felt
Fame rationed thin among so many clients –
Not many ways of wearing badge and belt,
Not many giants in a world of giants.
    I fear that Georges made some slight contribution
    To his untimely, unfair dissolution.

Blame him not much! O wish him what has brightened
Per saecula saeculorum Adam's race:
Life new-attained, limbs lissomed, conscience heightened,
The same old Georges with godhead in his face.
This for the present must be left mere wish,
And would have been the same if he had stayed
Along the streets of Calais hawking fish
Or where he was before the trumpets brayed.
There are whom I could blame with keener zest
Although his grave is such a garden now –
Vicarious heroes from whose mighty breast
Fumed the hot air that made those trumpets blow,
    Fishers of men with nets of strange device,
    Established in gold letters – at this price.

Ideals, after all, in noble states
Are necessary as the petrol pump;
While the great public slaves to pay its rates,
Someone must elevate the frowsy lump,
And from the rut of commonplace prosperity
Cry up adventurous passion, since elsewhere
Masked in most loathed fair-seeming of sincerity
Satanic synods, hand to hilt, prepare.
How sweet is power, one mind's command how sweet!
The patriot with his pencilled slips may feel
His headlines booming down the distant street
And shedding influence on each cottage meal.
    That Georges was gullible his chums admit,
    Or would, but have forgotten him and it.

Tyrtaeus led the way; the bards since him
Have done their best with martial strains to sunder
Georges, Hans, Bill, Carlos. Couched where goldfish swim,
They sing for glory: 'There's a sound of thunder
Afar,' to meet which tempest they approve

That every citizen should grasp a rifle,
In the direction of the thunder move,
Rush on the foe, transfix him. Death? a trifle.
Thus lyric genius ever stooped to cheer
The march that ends in billets under clay,
Melodious metres helped the lance and spear,
And should have stopped what came the other way.
    Love thou the poets. Georges even when he fell
    Had word from them: 'See, what a lovely shell.'

Is War so subtle, that of his machine
So meagre and absurd a wrack survives?
Or is Peace wise to clothe with such gay green
That spasmal visnomy whose menace thrives
The more, the less regarded or reported?
Assume which way you please, one thing is sure:
The face of Peace was hardly more distorted
By War's acids and axes than is War
Veiled from the sense by Peace. His metals die
Faster than skulls of those they struck to pieces;
A decade after, you may peer and pry
For strands of wire, for mortars whose caprices
    Made your days years, for shaft and iron emplacement.
    Vain search – to find inscrutable Effacement.

Perhaps the acres that have staged event
Will yield some whisper of it, might we hear.
Immense endeavour, tragic tournament,
History's smithying should not disappear
Without reverberation. Battle flames
With other ardours than of bursting shells,
And many a gray surviving soldier claims
That strange excitement surges nowhere else.
Walking past Mont Saint Jean I caught a drift
Of Waterloo's red crisis, and have known
Suspense and worse and felt the barrage lift
In even vaster battles of our own;
    Yet I have wandered stranger worlds than those,
    Planes which whoever dreams intensely knows.

Verbrandenmolen's windmill likes the breeze
That flies across this farmland; the bright toil
Is as it should be. Why alone are these
Condemned? But not these only, save we foil
The sails and cogs of other, uglier mills

Whose masters even keener wait each gust,
And beckon to false shapes of golden hills
Where Adam's seed may be ground down to dust.
Arise, young spirits, and march in pride, but not
Against your kind; attack at dawn, and capture
Line after line – but fire no single shot
Except of progress, and run through with rapture
   These old, gross demons: Rumour, Ignorance,
   Advantage, Spite, Conceit and False Romance.

That victory will be won, if I may trust
A thought that steals about this place, so mute
Upon what lately raged here. This poor just
Ranked soldierly, these veterans salute
The promise; the old guard presenting arms
Trusts to the new, and gives it all it can.
Pointing at twinkling spires and big-barned farms
They smile a little. 'As the thing began
It ended; only, as you see, we boys
Have copped unlucky, and the C.O. too,
But he'd just had *his* leave; well, all that noise,
And all us millions as they say *napu*.'
   Thus a dim music every step I tread
   Connotes the living purpose of these dead.

No particular cemetery is alluded to. These stanzas were originally included in the volume by several authors entitled *Challenge to Death*, published by Messrs. Constable.

[*Challenge to Death*, London, Constable, 1934
Poems 1930-1940, January 1941]

In My Time

TOUCHED with a certain silver light
In each man's retrospection,
There are important hours; some others
Seem to grow kingfisher's feathers,
Or glow like sunflowers; my affection
In the first kind finds more delight.

I would not challenge you to discover
Finally why you dwell

In this ward or that of your experience.
Men may vary without variance.
Each vase knows the note, the bell,
Which thrills it like a lover.

When I am silent, when a distance
Dims my response, forgive;
Accept that when the past has beckoned,
There is no help; all else comes second;
Agree, the way to live
Is not to dissect existence.

All the more waive common reason
If the passion when revealed
Seem of poor blood; if the silver hour
Be nothing but an uncouth, shot-torn tower,
And a column crossing a field,
Bowed men, to a dead horizon.

[*London Mercury*, Vol. 33, No. 195, January 1936
An Elegy, November 1937]

Cabaret Tune

I CAN'T go back to Then.
    You can't go *back* to Then.
And I wish I might; but do I wish right?
Where really shines that alluring light
    Which from Now would decoy to Then?

I have gained so much since Then.
    You have gained *so* much since Then.
Would that bloom on the wheat, if one might retreat,
Be worth the rest? would the fresh dawn-sweet
    Encounter justify Then?

God knows, Now would always be Then.
    God *knows,* Now would always be Then.
The flash of the brook and the life of the look
And the scent of the may and the charm of the book
    Move for ever between Now and Then.

[*An Elegy*, November 1937]

Anti-Basilisk

BUT for a Basilisk who somewhere cowers
Camouflaged under artful shade,
Our siege would prosper; we have guns enough,
Valour enough, and seldom sleep.
Still, when a Basilisk is on their side,
It makes some difference. That unnatural eye
Poisons our knighthood, drops our petals dead,
Yet nothing seen of outward wound or scathe.
Nor, though our best observers dawn to dusk
Explore the city walls from rick and ridge,
Can we discover in what casemate squats
The Basilisk: which, so, might be impossible,
Since he who meets that look, that silent line
Of death, must join the rest of our poor lads
For whom the chaplain opens his prayer-book now.
It must be otherwise contrived.
So, gentlemen, after prolonged discussion
With all our centenarians, I resolve
As follows: At midnight to-night
Between our foremost works and those proud walls,
The Royal Engineers and special troops
Will hoist, lift, raise and generally erect
A turret; on that turret they will fix
One mirror (now arriving from the Base),
Confronting with its large and lustrous round
The Basilisk where he, perhaps, is found.
It is a perfect stratagem – we hope;
Let people hang themselves with their own rope.
The theory we are working on is this;
Basilisk eyes the glass. The glass at once
Shoots back his baleful stare. It cannot miss.
He dies self-poisoned. What? No, no, good dunce;
Here's someone asking if a Basilisk
Has some precaution against such a risk;
Well, gentlemen, to dinner, or to horse –
At sunrise we shall take the town, of course.

[*An Elegy*, November 1937]

Present Discontents

SEEKING no more
The auguries of to-morrow's peace or war,
I can think only of to-day in terms
That no 'great journal' ridicules or confirms.
    This sky and earth
In my impression certainly seem worth
Some hours of my concern, and maybe yours;
Rooks, peewits, herons I consult to-day,
If I can find them in the glades and moors,
And if they have some truths to flash my way.
    Should they say no,
I do not doubt some coral-berried tree,
Slenderest and finest she where many grow,
Will well contrive to catch me suddenly.
    And mark that tower
High on the ridge, cool-lighted and austere;
As if I never before imagined power,
His quiet domination fills me here,
While long, long centuries throng my tiny hour,
And the lark cries to the sun – in this or any year.

[*Oxford Magazine*, Vol. 55, No. 5, 12 November 1936
An Elegy, November 1937]

'Can You Remember?'

YES, I still remember
   The whole thing in a way;
Edge and exactitude
   Depend on the day.

Of all that prodigious scene
   There seems scanty loss,
Though mists mainly float and screen
   Canal, spire and fosse;

Though commonly I fail to name
  That once obvious Hill,
And where we went and whence we came
  To be killed, or kill.

Those mists are spiritual
  And luminous-obscure,
Evolved of countless circumstance
  Of which I am sure;

Of which, at the instance
  Of sound, smell, change and stir,
New-old shapes for ever
  Intensely recur.

And some are sparkling, laughing, singing,
  Young, heroic, mild;
And some incurable, twisted,
  Shrieking, dumb, defiled.

[*English*, [January] 1936
An Elegy, November 1937]

On a Picture by Dürer

Sonnenuntergang

WHERE found you, Dürer, that strange group of trees,
That seared, shamed, mutilated group still standing
To tell us *This is War*: where found you these?
I did not guess, when last I saw shells landing
Smash on the track beside, how old they were.
They had been good tall pines, I saw, but not
Of such great bole as argued they stood there
When your antiquity might pass the spot.

A thousand of us who as yet survive
From what was modern war the other day
Could recognize them, killed in the great Drive
Which strewed so many bones in glory's way.
But, you, your date was wrong. From which of your towers
Saw you that night across the centuries,

164

Under that cloud with baleful eye-slits, ours –
Our sign, our shape, our dumb but eloquent trees?

[*Miscellany*, August 1936
An Elegy, November 1937]

Recurrence

FAIL me not, flying angel, when I come
To the great bend in the road, the hill's descent
Through ten thousand trees; O be not dumb
But with your glorious shout, that with me went
Invincible that way, amaze afresh
A wanderer, magnify those glittering drops
Of cold quick rainstorm challenging tired flesh,
Until all enmity and difference stops,
And I am strong with them. Fail not at all
When past those grieving trees the fated road
Sinks into swamps where half a yard of wall
Pretends man lived here once who stacked and sowed;
And from that wayless saeculum of despond
O, will you lift to the flashing heights beyond?

[*An Elegy*, November 1937]

Tell Your Fortune

(Written for the reunion of the Southdown Battalions, 1936)

THIS was my pleasant dream, not ten days past:–
Another War had broken out at last;
But not the kind of War that H.G. Wells
Or many another jovial scribe foretells,
Nor altogether like our own affair,
And yet it had a drift that took me there.

I found myself still groping up our road
Through *Festubert*. The Verey lights still glowed
Thin green on the eastern skyline, and I saw
The *Brewery* ruin again, and felt like straw;

165

But then the night that had mantled dank and raw
Became blue summer morning, and I found
Some Southdowns sauntering in a meadow ground,
Thistled and ragged, but a fairy place,
And I knew many a voice, and many a face –
And by the road a garden, that had been
Shelled once, was a startling miracle of green,
And half-wild trees and bushes by the gate
Bore such rich fruit, so thronged, so bloomed, so great
That I could hardly tell myself this way
Led to *Canadian Orchard*! Fain to stay,
Yet on I went, as dreamers must; at length
I met the old Battalions in main strength,
And they were holding the *Old German Line*.

– Bless me, that was no trouble. Wit and wine
Were hurrying round, – there stood a vast marquee
Where all could get lobster or chicken free,
And sergeant-majors playing harps invited
All ranks to drink, and dance and feed. – 'Delighted!'
Commanding officers came tripping neatly,
The G.O.C. took wine and warbled sweetly,
The sun shone golden on this brotherhood,
And Quartermasters sighed 'I will be good.'
Mules at the transport lines across the way
Expressed harmonious thanks for purple hay,
And scores of angels, fluttering through our ranks,
Placed in each honest paw ten thousand francs.
Alas, I woke; but then it struck me, This
Was not a mere imaginary bliss:
It was a forecast of this annual *Do*,
And here you are, to prove my vision true.

[*Southdown Battalions' Association Annual Dinner*, 28 March 1936.
An Elegy, November 1937]

Stanzas: Midsummer, 1937

O ENGLAND! lose not now, O never lose
   The only glory that is worth endeavour;
The times are doubtful, and the task to choose
   Desperately hard: but they have seemed so ever.

CAN YOU REMEMBER?

Men before now, staring into their age,
    Finding it baffling, have proved masterful.
Be of their line; prepare for the turned page
    Of outcome by the present scanned in full.

Reckon prosperity as a fleeting dance.
    Grudge not adversity, for that unveils,
That counts the real wealth; yet if it chance
    That England long advance with swelling sails,
Then be not proud; even Death, as English Donne
    Interpreted long since, should not be proud;
Be unbeguiled. Measure not by the ton
    The wealth of nations. Mark each golden cloud.

How every country makes report of you,
    My country! with such attitude of praise
As Gibbon's Rome at high tide never knew.
    Envy herself but offers you the bays.
Speak then with love and knighthood of each fact
    Or project or desire of human good
In other nations; nothing thence detract.
    Be the true best by you best understood.

Too long, committed to such loyal course
    As even successful mummery claims from you,
You follow forms which must beget remorse.
    O England, cozened? Let old zeal renew.
If indolence were named a hanging crime,
    What thousands of us should be shortly sent
To execution! Mercy gives us time,
    And we may yet see what our cat-naps meant.

Arise then, and delight shall march with gain;
    Know what is honest, what is sly uncover.
Be what you have been; *English* is no stain;
    England has many an unexpected lover.
The clearness of the windows of the soul
    Men often sought and often found as yours.
Blue-eyed and lustrous, beautiful and whole,
    Prove now your bright Shakespearean sense endures!

[*An Elegy*, November 1937]

ECHOES FROM THE
GREAT WAR

The Spell of France

LITTLE enough of that wide country
  Though fascinated long
Have I as yet acquired: that little
  Is constant undersong,
Astonishment, rest, recognition,
  In my life's round;
And whether I will or no my silence
  Reverts to that bright ground.

First, was it? from the verse of poets
  Who intimate and shy
Unveiled the squares, the fairs, the lovers
  Under that calm blue sky,
I thought I won some understanding
  Of the different lure
And look and consonance of life there,
  – And those first dreams endure.

Thereafter, currented with million others
  To history's roaring weirs,
I still found moments, and lacked not feelings,
  Some hours of smiles or tears,
To taste the elixir of that country,
  To kiss the garment's hem,
And, hurled away no matter how fiercely,
  To hoard more than one gem.

Thus now it comes, and from blest occasion
  Of later date though brief,
That some deep music from that country
  Shakes me like a leaf,
And the happy storm of dreams or pictures

169

Origined there
Will occupy my whole existence
   And seem my native air.

What else would you, could I? Endeavour
   To number and right-dress
The outward tokens of this passion
   Would be but foolishness:
To name (though sweet the names) each city,
   And village of that dream,
Each woodride, each château, each rampart,
   Quarry and cliff and stream;

To summon up lost children's laughter,
   And farmers' terse good talks,
Cassock and sermon in gaunt cool churches,
   Golden past-harvest walks,
Dry veterans garrulous at small tables,
   Bugles and horns and bells –
How might I by these hints create you
   Lord of my spell of spells?

[*Etudes anglaises,* Vol. 1, No. 2, April-June 1937
An Elegy, November 1937]

Rue des Berceaux

GLIDE beneath those elms, lost lane,
   Run away from forge and inn,
Seek the wide wheat-blazing plain,
   Cross silvering brook and climb to win
The hilltop with the far view
   Of spire and chimney, wood and lake,
And, sweet lane, take me with you,
   We'll start ere summer morning break,
Or when the winter pours amain
His dark slashing rain.

Never in this world again,
   Nameless byeway, shall we go
Shyly through the poppied grain,
   Where the young stream sang below;

And hardly may I tell now
   How much of you my fancy maps,
And if the sign would still show
   The place you made for once perhaps;
I thought I knew you, but the brain
Fights dream-time in vain.

Quit those puzzled streets, that slain
   Church of shattered saints, cleft tombs,
Take me with you, kindly lane,
   Freed from those close walls and glooms –
But what have you to haste for?
   The new bells chime, the new roofs glow,
And ghosts of an extinct war
   Would scarcely find a stone they'd know;
I dare this much: they'd bear some pain
Your strange grace to gain.

[*An Elegy*, November 1937]

Nights Before Battle

MOVING through those nights
   Of sad immense unknowingness,
Led by dodging lights
   Of pale disordered power,
Men through gulfs and heights
   Of outward fact and inward, press
   Towards the centre of their fate,
   The phantom top and tower.

Never was a Folly
   So built, so conjured; they would force
Mule-train, truck and trolley,
   Wear their young bones sore
To lift fierce Melancholy
   Into the skies, that rained of course
   Interminable objections to
   This thundering at God's door.

[*An Elegy*, November 1937]

171

Nearing the Ancre Battlefield, 1916

THE leafiest trees we ever saw,
  The most refreshful shadow they
  Had ever cast on a hot highway,
The only houses without flaw;
Life's look, a final look, all pure
To venturing boy or man mature;
But then, the loneliness, that shroud
Which, more than pack and gun, kept bowed
And isolated all our crowd!
For from no step nor window here
Woman's wit chose cavalier,
And never from the smithy rang
The shoesmith's fiery friendly clang,
Nor under eaves nor under oak
A labourer sat to snore or smoke;
All was so natural, up to here,
That these negations hardly proved
We came into the land of fear;
And slowly on the column moved.

I see the blue-white finger-post
Pointing to places five miles off,
Names that might make all Hades laugh,
Accessible as Banquo's ghost.
A mile away – perhaps alive
We'd get that far that night; but five!
The moment stays; the twisted gate,
The well, the château wall;
And one green tree, profuse, elate,
Still canopies the moment great
With nothing or with all.

[*An Elegy*, November 1937]

172

Marching Back to Peace, 1916

HOW came such minutes, such inimitables
To lose their oneness? Was the sun so lazy,
The night so somnolent? The world so hazy?
Revive yourself, friend Willingness; find chronicles
For every form and organism we passed
That winter morning – none could go unglassed
In consciousness so ready, so released;
Or were you all as folk who flock to a feast
Whom expectation makes unable
To view more than the silver-selfish table?
But all was banquet then,
Even granite pavement paining the dim tread
Had glory in it, that the foot pained was not dead,
That those about, behind, before, were men –
How long? But did we pose, and did we deal
With that bleak query, short and stinging?
So, strike up, band, and clamorously conceal
That road, that new-found light; we are safer singing.

[*An Elegy*, November 1937]

Monts de Flandre

WHEN you were young, you saw this puzzling scene:–
There a deep plain spread, where a sudden flash
And sulky thunderous boom, or a storm of these,
Declared the war that trenched and tunnelled there.

Perhaps you had dragged your limbs from the painful centre
Of this denatured gunland, and had left
Something much like yourself in a shroud blanket
Next men who still cleaned rifles, stood to arms.

Then you had climbed clear of that solemn waste
Up the firm hill, the bastion of dear life,
And when the redeeming road had risen enough
You could believe you had been lucky again.

173

So, marching on, or jolted in a waggon,
The last explosion gone, like famine rescued
You ravined down the circumstance of peace
In the highland, every hovel, beck and bush.
How wonderful that line 'tween heaven and hell!
Was this a shrine? then why should you not kneel?

But wise are those, who, no such contrast needed,
To-day perceive that on those wooded hills
Something primeval and perennial waits,
And someone sings of an immortal chance.
Wise are the later lovers of those hills:
They will forgive war's ghosts, who also loved.

[*In Elegy*, November 1937]

In May 1916: Near Richebourg St. Vaast

THE green brook played, talked unafraid
    As though like me it gladly quitted
The shabby, shattered zones of fire
    With barbed wire webbed, with burnt scars pitted.

It was my hour, and sunset's flower;
    Now I could breathe and shed my trouble;
The track even here had danger in it,
    And the next farm lay a heap of rubble.

So being alone, my last job done,
    I followed the course of that lithe water
Westward in blossoming waywardness,
    Such beauty neighbouring so much slaughter,

With ray and song beguiled along;
    It seemed the war, for all its cunning,
Had missed this orchard brook, or some
    Especial fortune kept it running;

Half scared at this, something amiss,
    I doubted whether curst illusion

174

Had seized my brain and lured me on
To some intolerable conclusion;

So paused, went back to the general track,
The safer way for soldiers' walking:
And as the stream's last murmur stilled,
Our sixty-pounders started talking.

[*Poems 1930-1940*, January 1941]

Rhymes on Bethune, 1916

OLD town of France, the wish to walk
Your friendly streets had been our talk
In roofless barns, in rat-run saps,
Among war's most heart-piercing shapes;
Our dead companions, they would speak
Of you, and smile, 'Perhaps next week –
Perhaps next week I'll go on leave.'
Faint visions, that did not deceive.
We, not struck down, dared not much think
Why all of us stood on the brink,
That should have been the safe highway
Towards Life's gardens sweet with May:
And not a man declined, Bethune,
Your most politely offered boon:
An art of life precise and keen,
Flowers on the table, *bonne cuisine,*
And, after nights in trench and keep
Sleepless, serene sweet-valanced sleep.
O that was blessing, that was luck,
Four miles from fire-steps, mines and muck,
To see a church not yet a wreck,
To enter the bank and cash a cheque;
And as my memory tells the tale,
No distance from the green canal,
From the inn window, still I see
My old platoon acclaiming me,
The old platoon, or some of them,
Enjoying life, which dolts condemn,
At the corner of a Rue whose name
They can't quite get, but like *quand même;*

175

They woo me to their kind retreat,
With song and joke and cognac neat.

Leaving these boys I find my way
Where light winds in young lime-trees play
Along a pink but modest street,
While evening light falls sad and sweet.
Here I shall lodge, and here I find,
However critically inclined,
Two sisters, teachers, will not rest
Till they have lodged me 'attë best,'–
As shy and gentle as wood doves these
Reveal their wish to set at ease
A scapegrace boy whose scanty French
Is all he brings from Auchy Trench.

Why should I now so yearn to know
Just what they said, so long ago?
To put on canvas, pale and bright,
The countenances that smiled that night?
If only I could cause to flower
Afresh that happy vanished hour
When, hardly mentioning the great war
That ravined just beyond their door,
These ladies stayed shamelessly late
In consultation and debate
With one outlandish, whom as guest
They welcomed to their timid nest!
I cannot *see* them now, I grieve
To fail in this. Let Time upheave
His oldest citadels: he can.
He hunts me out of all my plan.
But spite of him, if I may speak
As a not wholly cracked antique
In Paradise, I'll claim for these
Two ladies Learning's best Degrees,
And should exult did they in turn
Desire to see my cobwebbed urn.

[*Poems 1930-1940*, January 1941]

176

Near Albert-Sur-Ancre, 1916

AT the foot of the church-tower I noticed some weeds,
Dock, henbane and nettle, a dusty crew,
And still the dust flew
From the lorry-wheels passing: I noticed some weeds
In the angle between
The tower and the nave, where weeds always had been.

The church was a skeleton, but just at that date
There was nothing going over. The Line had moved on.
A vast autumn day in immensity shone;
My errand was easy, my business could wait.
While I leisured it so, from the verge of the street
Those scruffy old weeds in a flash had me beat.

It was one of those corners behind a great war
Where nature had skulked like a spider or mouse,
Appalled but persisting; just room and no more;
Overlooked when the huge broom was sweeping the house;
Now shine, my dead garland, and while the fates trample
The best we had blossoming, be you my example.

[*Poems 1930-1940*, January 1941]

The Camp in the Wood

Somme Battle, 1916

DESPERATE wood, your skinny trees
   And unmossed clay
Have found green grace again to please
   To-day
Any who may be going your way.

Little did you once please me;
   I saw you undersized and gray,
And a beanstick's not my favourite tree;
   Our menaced stay
Within your bounds was misery.

The skies were sullen, our past
    And future looked like these.
The skies were louring and cast
    Steel rains sharp and fast
On tents and tracks and trees.

Then those stupid guns,
    Enormous, in the sandpit denned:
Still their savage good-evening runs
    In memory, still their big mouths send
Horrible hate to Huns:

Which name recoiled to me
    And with deep trouble thronged my soul,
And marshalled ultimately
    The way it would not: such control
But fathered liberty!

Thus to me in the vale of years
    Holy almost and serene
Martinsart Wood appears.
    May you be fresh and green,
Dear coppice, when Doomsday nears!

[*Poems 1930-1940*, January 1941]

To a Nature-Lover

YOUR cry is 'Back to Nature'; we
    Whole-heartedly agree.

In nineteen-sixteen we emerged
From front-lines high-explosive-scourged,
Knowing we had some days ahead
    Of life in quiet country.
High summer's vivid dome for days
Roofed our whistling singing ways,
And south we marched without affrays
    And camped with hardly a sentry.

It might be some old water-wheel,
Some rivulet twining like an eel,
Some lonely elm – the old appeal
   Struck home among us slogging.
Great national forests seemed our lovers,
Gladly would we have tried those covers,
In every heath we wished manoeuvres,
   But orders allowed no lagging.

What longing filled us while we trod
With footsore rhythm each tumbril-road,
And passed the quarryman's tramline load
   And saw the harvest thronging!
Each cockerel flamed with our own fire,
Each thatched roof housed our kind desire,
We stared from furrow to barn and spire
   With a most natural longing!

[Formerly 'Echoes from 1914-18'.]

[*St. Martin's Review*, No. 597, November 1940
Poems 1930-1940, January 1941]

Ruins

BE swift, the day will soon be here,
And I don't quite see why scramble out
Of safe or fairly safe C.T.'s
To smell out useless heaps like these;
Be quick then, for the daylight's near,
And God knows what this game's about.

We sprawled up out of Something Road,
And trenches for a moment seemed
A dream's false-fluttering episode;
Beneath our feet a true road gleamed.
Beside us railings, gardens, gates
Shattered but recognized appeared,
Givenchy's prim snug villadom,
Which Worley half admired, half feared.

The least destroyed might still preserve
Lines of a windowed wall, red roof.

The battlefield's appalling curve
Coiled round, with flaming bursts for proof,
Doom's maw! but sense of love and kind
Still rose to us as we prowled that street,
And we were mutely glad to find
Such answer to our indiscreet
Adventure.

         Grayness rushed to light,
And animal-like we hustled down
To sandbagged workings, and that night
With countless others was all gone.
But still it beats the shocks and shellings
That we responded, had a mind
To walk among those gun-flogged dwellings
And keep in touch with something kind.

[*Poems 1930-1940*, January 1941]

Farm Behind Battle Zone

GENTLE, dark day, and country tracks,
    Houses as yet unhurt,
I saw you and I feared the axe
    Invisible and curt
Which from that heaven of hellish chance
    Would lay you in the dirt.

But chicken pecked about, and sows
    Grunted across the yard,
And willows with pin-cushion boughs
    Stood on their usual guard;
Madame was making lace, Louise
    Writing a picture-card.

I cannot count the hours, that passed
    With that farm menaced so,
Of which I saw some few; the blast
    Of war at length laid low
Each tile and lath, each pane and latch
    Of the quietest farm I know.

[*Poems 1930-1940*, January 1941]

Company Commander, 1917

'HOW lovely are the messengers that preach us the gospel of peace.'
So sang my friend, the company commander, in the trough of war,
Amid interminable shocks and snags, expecting no release.
It was not irony that prompted his song; though the daily score
Of casualties was even at the moment employing his pen,
And though his ridiculous shelter could stop no missile more
Than an empty bully-tin, being the target of daily torrents
Of hissing shattering shells; yet no shell tore
Through VID.'s own armament; signing returns and warrants
He recalled old music, commanded, guarded, jollied his men.

'O for the peace that floweth like a river.'
That too he sang, and damned, at each pause, red-tabbed Brigade,
Whose orders for grimness more than the frost-spell made us shiver;
Through VID.'s mild music loomed some bomb-and-bayonet raid.
Dead lies my friend, the fighter, from whom I have rarely heard
Against a human enemy one unhumorous word.

[*Poems 1930-1940*, January 1941]

THE NEXT WAR

In the Margin

WHILE few men praise and hardly more defend
That armed power which from here, and as things are,
Appears the whole Japan; while this forced war
Inhuman drags to some inglorious end,
And kills, and fires, and fouls, I too must feel
Horror and wonder at the deeds thus done,
And fear each day's exploit of crashing steel
Has merely lost what old Japan had won.

But through the smoke and dust I still can see,
And may I not forget, much that belongs
To that great name 'Japan' as well as those.
Faultless devotions raise clear eyes to me;
Through crowded streets gray-headed virtue goes,
And from poor farms I hear old peaceful songs.

[*The Listener*, 26 January 1938
On Several Occasions, April 1939]

In West Flanders

Is it the light that makes the silence
Of this long lake, for silence rules –
Though many row, or walk the terrace –
The curving shores, the china pools?
Or perhaps that hill of many memories
That citadels it high beyond
The farthest osiers, casts a spell
On this not quite coeval pond?

The air is populous with voices,
And yet the moment that we strayed
From the highroad, tempted by the cloister
Of elms towards the watery glade,
We were not conscious of these voices
But of a calm, a lull, a still
Invulnerable world of silence –
O quiet sky and lake and hill!

This sluice allows a bubbling current
To slide beneath the sluiceman's loft,
But that faint rumour lasts a moment
And unimaginably soft
Dies; and the gay and sly exchanges
Of parties in the boats aswim,
Out there among the lingering lilies,
Leave silence like an angel hymn.

What read you there, at your small table,
Young beauty with the varnished nails?
I read a – well – Victorian novel,
I seldom read such solemn tales,
But, finding it while I was waiting
For Albert (fishing over there),
I found I couldn't leave off reading –
I think it's something in the air.

And you, friend landlord, and chance comer,
Buying a view-card and a bock,
What are you worrying out together?
Nothing, we hope, that you will mock.
The fact is, he and I were talking
Of carp and how they seem to know
A friend who gives them bread or cherries –
They live a hundred years or so.

But quietly here, among these willows,
This boy has made himself a lair,
And we will question him in whispers:
He shines and warns us, 'Please take care!
My friends the wood-mice might suspect us,
I'm from the town – but here she comes,
The wisest and I think the mother,
To carry off these dangerous crumbs.'

Such notes upon the verge of silence
Imperil that deep flood no more
Than does the polished lessening ripple
Shaped by the angler's gentle oar;
The autumn evening now impending
Changes the painted lake we found,
But our enchantment travels on,
A silver silence of sweet sound.

[*On Several Occasions*, April 1939]

Travellers, 193-

BRIGHT insolent winds assail the shores
    Of northern France, and the crested waves
Tilt at the miles of sands and shingles
    Where as yet no public misbehaves.

Pale painters get a trifle busy
    On the shut kiosks and blank cafés,
But as yet there's more suspicion than hurry
    And the wind will pound yet several days.

Wild scampering sunbeams show the city
    Is clamorous red and silver blue,
And straight-lined fortifications yield
    Part shelter, whence that coloured view.

Strong-elbowed and with wondrous beard,
    Whose statue's this? read who it is, Clare;
Who, I'll forget inside ten minutes,
    And I'll not forget you reading it there.

I wonder, I, the older traveller,
    What you and John are taking back, –
Nothing maybe of my perceptions;
    A different series, another tack.

The wind may sing his sea-song later
    In your review as he will in mine,
The coast of England gloom and glitter
    To you as to me: so the moment shine,

185

It will be enough, for watching you meeting
    With foreheads smooth this sharp clean day,
I feel at once deep joy and trouble,
    And winds blowing each a separate way.

[Formerly 'Travellers 1938'.]

[*Times Literary Supplement*, 31 August 1940
Shells by a Stream, October 1944]

'Age 200'

At an Old Comrades' Dinner

'JUMP to it,' roared a thunderous voice; 'Fall in,' another bawled;
'Take his name,' a third barked out, and I was duly hauled
Before the most enraged C.O. who ever yet appeared.
'H'm, Pumpkin, what have you to say? Parading with a beard? '

'A beard? I crave your pardon, sir, but if I might make bold,
This hairy frieze is natural to the very very old.'
'Old! what's your age?' 'With deference, sir, I can't precisely say;
It must be quite a hundred, rather two, if it's a day.'

'Come, come – the man has lost his wits. A hundred?' 'Colonel, yes;
I venture, with respect, to state this is no idle guess.
Do not, dear sir, be petrified by what I now advance:–
You formerly commanded us in the mud of North-East France.'

'God bless me, so I did. Of course. It all comes back. Say on.'
'O how your troops could dubbin boots, how every buckle shone!
And, if I'm right, each Sunday night we scrambled through the mud
Of various parts of Belgium athirst for Teuton blood.

'I can't recall quite when that was, but I am almost sure
That this was in the period which they used to call The War.
For other points occur to me, there was one special trick
Of scratching holes and – trenches, yes – with shovel and with pick.

'And things kept dropping here and there, which tended to explode,
And rum was issued, but this rum might loiter on the road.'

186

'Gadzooks,' the Colonel answered. 'Case dismissed! The rascal's right.
We must all be quite two hundred. Well, we'll celebrate to-night.'

[*Southdown Battalions' Association Annual Dinner*, 5 March 1938
Poems 1930-1940, January 1941]

To W.O. and His Kind

IF even you, so able and so keen,
And master of the business you reported
Seem now almost as though you had never been,
And in your simple purpose nearly thwarted,
What hope is there? What harvest from those hours
Deliberately, and in the name of truth,
Endured by you? Your witness moves no Powers,
And younger youth resents your sentient youth.

You would have stayed me with some parable,
The grain of mustard seed, the boy that thrust
His arm into the leaking dike to quell
The North Sea's onrush. Would you were not dust.
With you I might invent, and make men try,
Some genuine shelter from this frantic sky.

[*On Several Occasions*, April 1939]

The Same Englishman

AMONG these boys (and they were sound
And generous all as may be found
In any of this world's societies)
One especially caught my mind,
Who frequently had striven to find
The else forgotten harsh anxieties
Undergone by the boys I saw,
Much like these same round the evening lamp,
Involved in huge distorted war
And dying in a tremendous camp.
With equal mind, with special sight,

187

With his interpretation right,
This youth long afterwards had made
(As later speech would state) the grade,
And by his spirit newly empowered
In scenes where I myself had cowered
From flying and upheaving hell,
I knew the dead and missing fell
Not unrewarded; where he goes,
I see a tough platoon of those.

[*On Several Occasions*, April 1939]

At My Writing Table

UNQUESTIONING I follow – follow whom?
That sounds like questioning, and I have found
It makes no difference. Ghosts will shift their ground;
Then either take their hint, or give them room.

That pond in sultry midnight just beyond
The last pale house of a township in Japan,
What can it mean to me or any man
Who once passed by it? Still I feel that pond.

But fast as ether's waves the sense is swung
To midnight Argentine, and every light
And every bell-voiced cricket make that night
Necessity to me; I move among

The radicals, the hot-heads at the den
Which ends the track; and eyes I see, which pierce
Mine and myself with problem; but transverse
The phantom has commanded me, and then

In the sour concrete hole the corporal shows
His muddy map, his Z Day zone of fire;
'This is the end of every man's desire';
Emerging there we see a winter rose

Of burning beauty on the hill ahead,
And fearful contours rush to that wild flame;

188

We cower in storms of steel, the flower-show game
Is played on us; up there they clear the dead.

At least this next arrangement kills less troops;
Lead, stranger, up an undistinguished road,
Where moth corrupts, and devilries corrode,
And, in meiosis, 'lovely woman stoops' –

So you have brought me to this midnight post
Where quiet reigns, and solitude writes books.
I yield; I can no other; habit looks
Stronger again. Adieu, return, my ghost!

[*On Several Occasions*, April 1939]

Exorcized

Written in October 1938

TWENTY years had nearly passed since the War called
    Great had roared its last,
And some were talking, men who fought the Somme
    before their twentieth year:
They talked of echoes, shadows, hauntings not so easily
    exorcized,
They granted Time had healed grim wounds, and yet
    these watchers recognized
        One stubborn and total fear.

'My dreams,' said one, and spoke for all, 'less frequently
    these nights recall
The clear-cut circumstance, the countless bitter facts
    familiar then
In gunpit, shell-hole, raid, patrol; the mud that swallowed
    gun, mule, man
Is seldom in my dreaming track, nor aid-post blood that
    piteous ran,
        Nor the dead in smashed-down den;

'But this it is which shatters sleep, and makes one's
    weary body leap:
Out of the gray uncertain dream this sentence speaks
    from shore to shore.

"The Armistice has all gone wrong. While we were
    out of the abyss,
It seemed heaven's mercy, faked you see merely to add
    new death to this:
        The War is on once more." '

Twenty years had nearly passed, and while these watched,
    they saw aghast
That giant enemy of sleep, that ghost which summed the
    worst they knew
Come creeping into waking thought, creeping and gather-
    ing like a storm
About the summer's loveliness, a vaster, more inhuman
    form.
        The dream was coming true.

Back to your madhouse, child of hell: too many of us
    know you well;
Infest our sleep, if thence we keep some record of your
    eyeless eyes.
But trespass not in the face of day. You find you cannot
    prowl this way;
Your very foulness forearmed those who now have
    checked your matinee,
        The generous, selfless, wise.

How things most complex, coiled and twined, simplicity
    may best unbind
Is no new secret; but till now it never showed so fountain-
    clear.
The meeting of four men as friends unhorses all the
    ancient fiends
Believing still the best will ever yield the best, as now it
    ends
        One swollen and final fear.

[*Times Literary Supplement*, 8 October 1938
Poems 1930-1940, January 1941]

War Talk: Winter 1938

THEY'RE talking of another war,
They say some things I've heard before,
They seem to me a shade too sure
    That they're the first, on this queer pitch.

I hardly know what words to use
To disenchant them of their views,
They've read their press, and they accuse ...
    And want to show they'll take the ditch.

This makes me call my old friends back,
To help me haunt my new friends' track.
I wish I had the artist's knack
    To win life-likeness from the past.

I'd have dear Daniells here just now,
And Wally Ashford here – 'and how!' –
And kindest Naylor: some pow-wow
    Would happen with so brisk a cast.

But they're all dead, and lots besides.
Where's Northcote? from our gaze he hides,
And French, the merry boy, abides
    With nothing, in some nameless grave;

Tice, son of duty, waits for us
In his neat-built sarcophagus;
Collyer is just anonymous,
    Our jester once, who lacked a shave.

If memory would not dodge me so,
There must be hundreds whom I know
Whose laugh would pace these boys, and slow
    Their haste to reach a wasteful end.

Unkind to us, ghosts mainly! worse
Unkind to their own cause and course,
For partial honour all perverse;
    But youth will always find a friend.

[*Poems 1930-1940*, January 1941]

To The Southdowns

At the yearly Reunion, 1939

TRUE, wars have not yet died out of the earth.
Some go day-dreaming still that bomb and shell,
Engines and legions topped and tipped with steel,
Will bring some glorious consequence to birth.
But you long since discovered, war is hell;
The men you fought against are of your mind;
Wise victory is yours and theirs to-day.
Through recent hours of crisis I could feel
This power of veterans quietly combined
To baffle danger, take the better way.

You, my old comrades, see the modern trend
Of men and manners hurrying from the past;
In new commotion it may often seem
That your far battles were a weary dream,
And your experience, once so fierce and vast,
Grown useless now. Be sure, that journey's end
Was not when you returned from fires of war;
You've that truth in you, learned in suffering then,
Which marches on, and secretly rules men,
And every year grows mightier than before.

Those whom we left in Flanders and beyond
Yet speak, and share the cause, and stand for peace;
New generations unawares respond
To their deep meaning; their effects increase.
We reassemble, and we have them here,
True-hearted, eager, just the men we knew;
And he who writes these words comes year by year
To show how much he owed to them and you.

[*Southdown Battalions' Association Annual Dinner*, 4 March 1939
Poems 1930-1940, January 1941]

The Sum of All

So rise, enchanting haunting faithful
Music of life recalled and now revealing
Unity; now discerned beyond
Fear, obscureness, casualty,
Exhaustion, shame and wreck,
As what was best,
As what was deeply well designed.
So rise, as a clear hill road with steady ascension,
Issuing from drifted outskirts, huddled houses,
Casual inns where guests may enter and wait
Many a moment till the hostess find them;
Thence ever before the carter, passing the quarries,
The griffin-headed gateways,
Windmill, splashing rill, derelict sheepfold,
Tower of a thousand years –
Through the pinewoods,
Where warm stones lodge the rose-leaf butterfly;
Crossing the artillery ranges whose fierce signs
Mean nothing now, whose gougings look like
Bird-baths now; and last, the frontier farm
And guard-house made of bracken.
Rising to this old eyrie, quietly forsaken,
You bear me on, and not me only.
All difference sheds away,
All shrivelling of the sense, anxious prolepsis,
Injury, staring suspicion,
Fades into pure and wise advance.
So rise; so let me pass.

[*The Listener*, 16 March 1939
Poems 1930-1940, January 1941]

A Window in Germany

August 1939

STILL the mild shower grows on; amid the drops
The gray gnats loiter or frisk; but we within
Like their sport less. So from my window here,
This ample casement built in the huge old wall
Which even a nunnery might find thick enough,
Barred with old iron branchwork monster-thorned,
I glance into the idle croft below.
I could not find a more familiar scene,
Known from my childhood, known to all my race –
The flagged path from the kitchen of the farm
Into the tousled orchard, plum and pear;
And under boughs of elder the stone sty;
The dog's dish which to-day he half forgets;
The nettles cluttering up the heaps of logs,
The raspberry-canes scrambling on leaning pales:
An English casual scene, which tells at once
Of rural mastery, and of rural ease.
Thus from my window here in Germany
The pleasant yard-scape shows. The world beyond
Is Sunday evening, and deserves its peace,
After the dogged action of the week,
The harvest battle fought into the night
With lanterns steady or marching; on whose heel
Tremendous thunder flamed and gunned for hours,
Bursting from Weser's vast black-wooded hills.
Such hills, such forests, even such confluent storm
Were not in my old haunt; but it is much
To find the kinship of this quiet house,
Where gentlest goodness lives and constant care,
And where, from many a nook, far-sundered ghosts,
To whom my ways mean something, gaze on me.

[*Times Literary Supplement*, 16 September 1939
Poems 1930-1940, January 1941]

About these Germans

HE who now speaks some verse to friendly minds
Once ventured words in praise of charming France;
Could venture further. Through this world he finds
A wealth of life to laud, to love. By chance

In Heidelberg a master of our tongue,
An equal friend of France and Britain, read
Those grateful rhymings, held them not ill sung,
And welcoming the rhymer, commented:

'I have some hope, you one day will compose
Lines of the same regard, the same approach
Towards Germany.' Remembering that disclose,
The rhymer sets his Moselwein abroach.

Let there be gathered in one social scene
Of Englishmen and Germans any score,
And spite of language, habit, will between,
Those men will part good friends. – We stand at war.

We – who? If war were fought by those who frame
The hideous goblins due to be destroyed,
The comic spirit might enjoy the game,
And it might gratify our unemployed.

But let digression hide her face. The match
In progress now has little use for her.
The bonfire, though its flame seem loth to catch,
Is nicely laid for millioned massacre.

Not the time now for cordial verse or wine
To flow between these lines of kindred folk.
Blot out those dreams of *morgensonnenschein*.
What is a bayonet for? The other bloke.

Still, he who now and ever prefers the speech
Of Shakespeare, Milton, Coleridge, Hardy, calls
On long remembrance; hears the flaming screech
Of war he knew between these nationals.

He sees their rival courages; admires.
Such men would fight a race of nightmares down.
Alike they stand beneath the dawn's drum-fires
Unshatterable of soul; alike are blown

To mist or muck; he sees, and sees much else.
O that our general sight would soon disband
The artifice which leads men to such hells.
There's no sworn enemy in that kind land

With all its clever cities and calm plains,
Markets and farms, forests and factories,
Big busy streams, broad highroads, lazy lanes,
Modern and mediaeval unities –

No final foe, graybeard or young blue eye,
Nor daily drive that tends except to good.
There's still the concept: Rather we would die
Than be perpetually misunderstood.

[*St. Martin's Review*, No. 587, January 1940
Poems 1930-1940, January 1941]

By the Belgian Frontier

'WHERE youth in fires
Fiend-blown, fiend-sudden, strove and fell,
The lilac sunlight plays like sweet desires,
The new leaves melodize, and the winds tune well,
The far tower's bell answers the browsing-bell.

'The twentieth year
Is now fulfilled, the lands of nourished strength
Warm-bodied give us welcome with their yield
Of flax blue-flowered and white. The placid length
Of the crystal lake lies like a war-god's shield,
Fallen for boys to find while flying kites afield.'

So even this spring
I wrote, I stared with never a wild surmise
Near that old frontier. Now the hideous thing
Is loose again, the ready death-forms rise.

196

[Formerly 'Dikkebusch'.]

[*Kingdom Come*, Vol. 1, No. 2, December 1939–January 1940
Poems 1930-1940, January 1941]

To Wilfred Owen

Killed in action November 4th, 1918

WHERE does your spirit walk, kind soldier, now,
In this deep winter, bright with ready guns?
And have you found new poems in this war?

Some would more wish you, with untroubled brow,
Perpetual sleep, which you perhaps wished once –
To unknow this swift return of all you bore.

And yet, if ever in the scheme of things
Past men have leave to see the world they loved,
This night you crossed the lines, for a second seen

By worried sentries. In vast tunnellings
You track the working-party; by the gloved
Wire-sergeant stand; look in at the canteen;

And I, dream-following you, reading your eyes,
Your veteran youthful eyes, discover fair
Some further hope, which did not formerly rise.
Smiling you fade, the future meets you there.

[*The Cherwell*, Vol. 58, No. 3, 3 February 1940
Augury, 27 April 1940]

Darkness

THE fire dies down, and the last friend goes,
The vintage matters no more now;
Tomorrow's development no man knows,
But that we have faced before now;
    The night comes on apace.

Darkness. Our revels, if that name serves,
Are ended. Now for the battle of nerves.
The embers cool, the jokes turn sour,
The local's lost, and hugest power
　　Comes prowling round the place.

But that's not new: there are older men
Who have been through that again and again –
There are children who will live to tell
The story of our stupid hell
　　To a fresh and charming race,

For whom the night shall never need
Our smoky shelterings, day succeed
Unpresaged with our wilful moods
Transformed into enormous broods
　　Of horror in dreadful chase.

　　　　　　　　　　　　　　early 1941

[*Eleven Poems*, March 1966]

A Survivor from One War
Reflects during Another

WHO, esteeming mankind
As his friends, as good people, most willing to be fair,
Could be free from invasions of daily despair,
To see their kind natures in cages confined,
And all their abilities bent to the work
Of torpedo, bomb, tommy-gun, bayonet and dirk?

Who, that formerly went
Through a weary war, still parched with its fire,
Would not in a new one at moments desire
To break Nature's law and pass self-sent
Into whatever after is destined for man,–
To leave the proved failure, and risk a fresh plan?

"End it when you will."
Loneliness, memory work for that call.
The hopes so high; so swift the fall!

198

And towards the next relief, what skill?
Yet where even Hamlet attained no decision
It will be well to wait larger vision.

    Selfishness dies at a flash
Of these aconites hurrying anew to the gleam
Of the mounting sun, and the eager stream;
At the voices of birds in elm and ash
Who, such is their song, take this living age
As the age of gold – every other, a cage.

[*Eastward*, March 1950]

AFTERTONES OF WAR

The Halted Battalion

ONE hour from far returns: Each man we had
Was well content that hour, the time, the place,
And war's reprieve combining. Each good face
Stood easy, and announced life not too bad.

Then almost holy came a light, a sense,
And whence it came I did not then inquire;
Simple the scene, – a château wall, a spire,
Towpath, swing-bridge, canal with bulrush-fence.

Still I, as dreamer known, that morning saw
The others round me taken with a dream.
I wondered since that never one of them
Recalls it; but how should they? We who draw
Picture and meaning are the dreamless, we
Are sentinels of time while the rest are free.

[Formerly 'The Halted Battalion: 1916'.]

[*Phoenix*, Autumn 1946
After the Bombing, October 1949]

The Hedgehog Killed on the Road

UNSPEEDY friend, poor earth-child, whose sad eyes
Seemed, when I met you creeping past in life,
To expect no luck from giants of other spheres,
I mourn you lying here; and in your shape
Coiled with vain skill for the last time, in your quills
Slackened and puny, see too deep resemblance
To other troubles, other reasonless

201

Downbursts of death, beyond your now dead brain,
And yet much like your own. Earth-child, these tears.

[*Civic Hall Quarterly*, March 1947
After The Bombing, October 1949]

Ballad of the Sergeants of Other Days

After Villon and D.G. Rossetti

TELL me now in what hidden way is
   Sergeant Garton, a Sussex Man,
And where the undrawn proficiency pay is
   Of gentle Roberts who 'also ran';
   Echo, for answer well you can
   Across the Ancre or Zillebeke pond,
   Tell me from keep, or from redan –
   Where are the sergeants, passed beyond?

Where now is calm good Arthur Davey
   Master of anti-gas device?
Lost to me in some trench wet-wavy,
   Found in the peace years once or twice:
   Similarly where's now that nice
   Observer Clifford who surely donned
   Uniform much as if yielding to vice?
   Where are the sergeants, passed beyond?

Unsted the quick-moving, clear-eyed Marshall,
   Great-hearted Worley of Worthing the pride,
My Wally Ashford astute and impartial,
   Seall of the runners, and Luck who plied
   With the rations up through the wild night-tide;
   Pell who so well in the aidpost conned
   Petty complaints, Rhodes the cooks' best guide–
   Where are the sergeants, passed beyond?

ENVOI

Colonel, enquire not – shall we scan
   This week or next with wishes fond

To spy in the everlasting plan
　　Where are the sergeants, passed beyond?

[Formerly 'Echo de l'Autre Guerre: a Ballad of the Sergeants of Other Days – after Villon and D. G. Rossetti'.]

[*Medical Bulletin*, Vol. 4, No. 1, January 1956
A Hong Kong House, September 1962]

At the Great Wall of China

PERCHED in a tower of this ancestral Wall,
Of man's huge warlike works the hugest still,
We scan its highway lashing hill to hill,
We dream its form as though we saw it all;
Where these few miles to thousands grow, and yet
Ever the one command and genius haunt
Each stairway, sally-port, loop, parapet,
In mute last answer to the invader's vaunt.

But I half know at this bleak turret here,
In snow-dimmed moonlight where sure answers quail,
This new-set sentry of a long dead year,
This boy almost, trembling lest he may fail
To espy the ruseful raiders, and his mind
Torn with sharp love of the home left far behind.

[*Times Literary Supplement*, 16 March 1956
Poems of Many Years, June 1957]

Frank Worley,
D.C.M.
July 1954

THERE was no death but you would face it
　　Even in your youth;
No riddle of life but you would grace it
　　With your brave truth.

To share, to give, to make privation
No trouble at all,
To honour all wise occupation
And duty's call,–

Such was your spirit, Frank, dear fighter
Foremost for peace,
Through whom even sunniest hours grew brighter
And dark thoughts cease;

To whom heaven gave reward best showing
Whereto you strove:
Old and young friendships overflowing
And a home of love.

[*Poems of Many Years*, June 1957]

Echo of War

ABOVE the torn-out town-end
A pale water-colour sky
And a dubious hour. The worst was by;
Suicidal guns were dumb,
The holes in the pavé all were made, time now
To fill them, when it was seen just how;
This town-end had been troublesome.
But here in some few months the child
Will run to school, will run from school,
And sunsets glow in many a jewel
On habit reconciled.
For me, ascending the miry, humpy track
Over the lifeless railway, in that slack
Mid-winter air, each house-wall left could stir
Long starved concerns of Peace, and the mere sense
Of curtains and cheap furniture
Transformed that shrivelled town-end
Into the shining city that's not far hence.

Echo of War I. Written 40 or more years after E.B.

[From manuscript.]

The Little Song

WHAT others overtake in wit's advance
The painters, poets, novelists of France?
Who else unite as they can all we know
Of life and dream of life, aloft, alow,
Amazing or amusing, who like these
Can see and show the world, so move, so please?
I wish that one of them had been with us
Through years of youth sun-flashed or sulphurous,
So now it might be merely, bring the book
And you may have – what now oblivion took.
    My mind tonight was drawn to such time past
By a French song, which was a quick light cast
On our young years, my friend of many now,
Siegfried; the song was trifling I allow,
But reawakened what those young years felt,
And tears and smiles and joys and sorrows dealt
So rapidly by fate: and how we went
At once much farther than the slow extent
Of life since then: so war led far beyond
The actual rootfield, crossroad, mill-knoll, brickyard pond
Where the Line ran, homes homeless, churches dead
Or dead tomorrow, amid the stupid bed
Blown into a treetop and the dead shell too
Fixed in the church-tower like a mollusc new.
What were we then? why such appalling strife
Fallen on our men and us in early life?
To those old questions even this song tonight
Told me the genius that could answer right,
As over life's whole scene the French observe,
Untrammelled, the report of brain and nerve,
Of grief and grandeur, love and fury giving,
Intent on all the tempest-calm of living.

[*A Hong Kong House*, September 1962]

205

Over the Valley

(An impression near Mont Kemmel, towards Bailleul, 1917)

TREMBLING blue, blent grey or green
Presented that vast valley-scene;
    A river-curve, a château shone.
    It was autumn evening, ages agone.

You and I knew nothing much
Of the region shown us: such and such
    Within it were, worked, wondered on;
    This was autumn owl-light, years agone.

The hill-grove, lately leafy lay
Next the descending waggon-way,
    And under, dimmingly, wide, thorpe-strown
    It was solemn landscape, look; long flown.

Then, what went there with winding course?
The amber-lanterned iron horse;
    But, a second look – his train was gone
    That autumn evening into the unknown.

Or was perhaps his the voice so shrill
And short below that shrouded hill?
    Whence other utterance, listen, soon
    Filled farmland's night air, years agone.

The breeze will flutter, from can you tell
What fields of sleep? – and sad night air
    Is sadder still, when the breeze has blown
    Through some bare branches, then is gone.

I liked that villa's misty lamp
Triumphant, tiny, defying the damp
    Ancestral autumn coming on;
    The permanence such far lamps had won!

Love-lit agreement and sweet desire
Could set even that lost dusk afire;

The curtained family-joy, even one
Signalled 'all's well' as shade marched down.

The rustling grove, the thrill-cold shower,
The ghost from the quarry, the path to No-where, –
Simple simplicities, the whole tone
Of an autumn nightfall dead and gone.

[*A Hong Kong House*, September 1962]

A Swan, A Man

AMONG the dead reeds, the single swan
Floats and explores the water-shallow under,
While the wet whistling wind blows on
And the path by the river is all alone,
And I at the old bridge wonder
If those are birds or leaves,
Small quick birds or withered leaves,
Astir on the grassy patch of green
Where the wind is not so rough and keen.

What happens to my thought-time,
To my desires, my deeds, this day?
The rainstorm beats the pitiful stream
With battle-pictures I had hoped to miss,
But winter warfare could be worse than this;
Into the house, recall what dead friends say,
And like the Ancient Mariner learn to pray.

1964

This little group was chosen from a number sometimes written after the day's work
of classes and committees in Hong Kong.

[Blunden has taken 'this group' from *Eleven Poems*, Cambridge, Golden Head
Press, 1966.]

Gone

WHAT happened to The Gun? a fine gun it seemed,
An eighteen-pounder gun which no doubt once gleamed
With the slashing rain of Flanders in the flashing battle-night,
And awhile in our old village had stood, lean and bright,–
Presented to the parish. Silent to moon and sun,
It stared out at the stockyards. What happened to The Gun?

Happenings in our village are soon enough talked round:
The darkest night can't hide them, the loneliest patch of ground
Has an eye to see, a tongue to tell. Good patriots are we,
And he who threatens England will be thrown into the sea.
But in some strange way that relic in mystery passed on;
The Elizabethan cottages look blank. The Gun is gone.

[*Eleven Poems*, March 1966]

Ancre, 1916

*Going up to the Line. It was a rainy night, and I was
surprised to see our shells flying over Thiepval Wood each
with a flash of light. The only time I remember that.*

For what reason I never can tell,
    But that one night over Thiepval Wood
A passing splendour belonged to each shell
    In its overhead journey, in multitude.
Flight upon flight, that flame-filled night,
Approaching the place, as in some new spell
Our rain-soaked company suffered affright.

Let the valley rest, let the trout-stream run
    As now other strangers report, along there;
Nobody lost and nobody won,–
    There is plenty of time, there's time to spare.
That night we trembled on some queer trail
That might make Christian himself turn pale.

[*Eleven Poems*, March 1966]

Armistice: A March

STILL in deep winter, the war country lies
Unveiled with winter's beauty, frost or snow;
The dull cloud moves not, colours will not rise
From far-off hill or close-by river's flow;
Are there inhabitants in this slow plain,
These silent groups of roofs all much the same?
So many spires can hardly point in vain,
But the drab cloud ignores each heavenly claim.

The afternoon is evening, night assumes
An earlier occupation than them both;
Track through trod root-fields clogging each inhumes
Intention and avail; desire quits growth,
And each becomes a weed-heap by the way.
There is no blast of ice and volley of sleet,
No numbing frost to end the dreary day,
But lightlessness was never more complete.

Thus trudging, thus supposing, the sad troop
That counted all those spires and ceased to count
And wondered if a farm could boast a coop
Or find an egg in all this plain's amount,
Were angelled; now, the latest light, a touch
Of sunset merely, told them all was well;
Their movement-orders had not lost them much
And just ahead what they had wished befell.

Into that hurt and puzzled city at last,
Dark as the night is, yet with lamps renewed,
The sons of sorrow, lame and hungry, passed; ...
Now more than ever needed fortitude,
The dull appearances above, around,
And unknown tasks ensuing,– winter then
As I remember, more than watched and frowned,
But what deep winter since destroyed those men?

[*Eleven Poems*, March 1966]

1966: S.S. Becomes an Octogenarian

ANOTHER era came while yet the last
Seemed worth our love, despite the pain it brought;
The Captain who had seen mad force aghast
And even alone defied it, deep in thought
Watched a new mystery, understood its vast
Quell of so much for which such millions fought.

Seer as he is – look in his face and know –
He seldom cursed the fates, but with his song
Made his comparisons of "long ago"
And these prodigious wonders, right or wrong,
In gratitude; youthfully he would show
Honour, affection, pastime loved so long.

Whose voice through battle-furies first had made
For me some lifting of the veil of war?
His, and from our own village! where he strayed
Valuing all virtues, even our vicar a roar?
Who afterwards upheld what I esssayed
In his own vein, and aided more and more!

But now the new phase strips our old home even
As foolish things, our concepts and our skills
Dead-born; but this will hardly be forgiven
By him the Captain, who through all fulfils
The old-style confidence in soul and heaven,
And with some wit awaits earth's daffodils.

[*Illustrated London News*, 19 February 1966]

Ancre Sunshine

IN all his glory the sun was high and glowing
Over the farm world where we found great peace,
And clearest blue the winding river flowing
Seemed to be celebrating a release
From all but speed and music of its own
Which but for some few cows we heard alone.

Here half a century before might I,
Had something chanced, about this point have lain,
Looking with failing sense on such blue sky,
And then became a name with others slain.
But that thought vanished. Claire was wandering free
Miraumont way in the golden tasselled lea.

The railway trains went by, and dreamily
I thought of them as planets in their course,
Though bound perhaps for Arras, how would we
Have wondered once if through the furious force
Murdering our world one of these same had come,
Friendly and sensible – 'the war's over, chum'.

And now it seemed Claire was afar, and I
Alone, and where she went perhaps the mill
That used to be had risen again, and by
All that had fallen was in its old form still,
For her to witness, with no cold surprise,
In one of those moments when nothing dies.

3 September 1966

[*Garland*, 24 May 1968]

APPENDIX

A BATTALION HISTORY

(with apologies)

THE Southdown Battalions' Association dines annually at the Brighton Aquarium, doubtless startling the regular inhabitants with its boisterous cheerfulness. At the last dinner something occurred which also startled me. It was publicly proposed, and so far as I could observe it was generally demanded, that I should write the history of one at least of these Southdown Battalions. In a spirit of mingled cowardice and devotion to duty I found myself rising to accept this 'onerous honour' (the evening was far advanced); and I now present my old friends with something which nominally tallies with their request. Unfortunately it is shorter than they expected, but the war was also shorter than they expected.

The 11th Royal Sussex Regiment, otherwise the First Southdowns, otherwise Lowther's Lambs (and of course the Iron Regiment), being composed principally of Sussex men, was formed at the outset of the war, but was not sent overseas until March, 1916. On March 5th the battalion landed at Havre. A week later, in the usual fashion of that period, it left billets in Morbecque for trenches at Fleurbaix, in which it received instruction from the Yorks and Lancs. The first casualty (a man killed by a bullet) happened in the communication trench on the way in. Within a year, those who could speak from experience of Fleurbaix, the convent wall, and the suspect farmer ploughing in view of the Germans with white or black horses on different occasions, were rare. The day after the début, possibly because of too conspicuous parades, some company billets in Fleurbaix were suddenly shelled with accuracy and the battalion lost sixteen men killed and wounded.

By March 20th the battalion, its rapid probation over, held a trench subsector by itself; after its four days there it emerged through quiet Estaires to Merville, then undamaged, and spent three weeks under training there. 'Training' made a considerable part of the war's burden. The battalion next marched through the plain southward to Hingette, a hamlet on the canal west of Bethune, well away from the trenches except for some primitive ones that intersected the fields, intended to be ready for some strange upheaval. An eastward move soon followed; billets at Gorre were quitted on April 19th and muddy trenches at Givenchy were taken over. Here the side-effects of the quarrels south of the Canal, in the grim contorted country by Loos, were felt and paid for in some casualties. May-day arrived, and that night the battalion was relieved. Among the willow-shaded lanes of Hinges by the Canal beyond Bethune, it passed several days; much cleaning-up, much *parlez-vousing*, and on one evening at least, the Band playing. Thence it marched away on May 9th to le Touret, in the rain, and from that straggling hamlet it supplied working-parties until on the 14th it relieved the 13th Royal Sussex in the moonlight along the breastworks of Festubert. A famous name! but May, 1916, was anything but the repetition of that dreadful one of the previous year, which had sown the marshy grounds we dug in with skulls and equipment. In this Festubert locality of snipers and machine-guns we manned our posts and patrolled and wired for almost a fortnight, and when the Hertford-shires had relieved us we returned hopefully to the Hingette cottages and lofts.

But suddenly on May 28th, amid fearsome rumours, the battalion was ordered up to the front line south of the La Bassée Canal, at Cuinchy, which was a 'hot shop'. Here it was that the first Military Cross was awarded to one of us (Lieut. H.S. Lewis), followed by the first Military Medals (to G. Compton and W. Booth); the action concerned had occurred in no-man's-land at Givenchy. The business of the trenches at Cuinchy was strenuous; heavy trench mortars fired often into us, and on June 3rd the Germans sent out a fighting patrol which only succeeded in bombing a few posts. Next night a mine was blown just ahead of our front trench; in spite of the miscalculation, the explosion and the savage shelling that immediately lit up the wet darkness cost us six killed and thirty-seven wounded. The battalion might have suffered even worse casualties had an unprepared raid on the fortifications opposite (which was to have been made by us) been attempted; but it is understood that Colonel Grisewood, at the price of being removed from his command, rescued us from this menacing plan. From the Cuinchy trenches we were withdrawn for the usual short rest at Annequin, a village of colliers and pigeons, and we came back early on June 8th in small parties. This front-line tour produced two more mines, one German, one (the more imposing) ours; these did us no harm; some bombing matches took place where the two trench systems almost joined. We were now promoted to the dignity of instructing the 8th Warwicks. During the night of the 11th an Argyll and Sutherland battalion took our place and we very wearily returned to Hingette.

North and south of the La Bassée canal were, and are, when you know them, different countries. We next went north again into the agricultural country, lay west of Neuve Chapelle for several days and at night were busy with picks, shovels and trench carpentering towards Richebourg l'Avoué. At midnight on June 21st we were relieving the 12th ('Second')

Battalion about Ferme du Bois, and in those breastworks and muddy ditches we remained until the 28th, when by daylight the Cambridgeshires came cheerfully in to relieve us and we were scattered in detachments among the keeps of Richebourg St. Vaast. Major G.H. Harrison about now succeeded to Colonel Grisewood, and for a time he had the continued services of Captain Wallace – a splendid soldier – as adjutant. Meanwhile, we were informed of the opening of the Great Offensive of 1916, and of a local share in it. Down the road, a canvas representation of a projecting corner of the German parapet, known as the Boar's Head, was rigged up, and our storm-troops were practised at it. The Boar's Head was to be bitten off on June 30th, mainly by the other battalions of our 116th Brigade; but from our battalion large parties were detailed for carrying and some bombing. We knew little of the aims of this attack, and in our view it appeared a much greater thing than it in fact was. It seems to have been intended to delay some German troops and artillery from their march south to the Sommeschlacht. The attack was advertised by a preliminary bombardment from our batteries on the afternoon of June 29th. We looked across at the flying woodwork and earthwork of the German line. On the next morning, while it was still dark, both artillery groups let fly (ours had a few seconds' start), and our infantry went over. The German machine-guns had no difficulty; the Brigade and the supporting pioneers and Engineers were massacred, our own casualties being one hundred and twenty killed, wounded and missing. Among the survivors were some, such as G. Compton, who had gone deep into the German lines almost alone.

Next afternoon, while this kind of thing was being enacted through miles and miles of Picardy, we were relieved and came to Lacouture, or the orchards that fringed it. We lived partly in light huts and the hours were punctuated by the fire of the heavies. On July 6th at night we were surprised to find ourselves marching south (and incidentally breathing tear-gas). We slept briefly at Beuvry (then a place that pleased us much), but next day advanced through the pale rain, in parties of six, along the stone highway east. The 4th King's Liverpools willingly made room for us in the trenches before Auchy, which were seldom free for an hour from the stinging blasts of all sorts of bombs and shells. Our casualties were all too many. This strain on the nerves lasted a week or so, and we were glad to be sent up to le Touret once more. On July 20th we held the Ferme du Bois line again, and on the 23rd a raiding party was sent across, but its failure cost us seven killed and wounded. Next day we side-stepped into the Festubert breastworks, and held them in high summer weather, when even the War took a siesta, until the 29th. It was daring to try a relief here in broad day but it came off, and we assembled after it at le Touret among the chicken-runs and estaminets. Then, to the general rejoicing, several days of billets in Bethune were given us. The people were kind and the food was cheap. Some may have visited the Red Lamp area, but not so many as would do in many War Books. After this holiday we occupied the trenches at Givenchy again, and made good use of the sunshine and the canal by bathing in the afternoons, about 200 yards from the nearest Germans. Some of these tried to fraternize one morning. Their opening joke was an allusion to bully beef and biscuits; but at that time we were well fed even in the trenches. On August 11th we left Givenchy for what had been long foretold – our part in the Battle of the Somme.

The period thus concluded was quite a distinct one. Throughout the battalion was seldom at any distance from the trenches – but the trenches were in the main 'truly rural'. Horrible and destructive moments occurred, yet there was something of beauty and of health in the general impression. You soon came into the scenes of ordinary life as you left the front line behind. The ruins of Richebourg St. Vaast, of Festubert and even of Cuinchy and Givenchy were substantial, and bits of architecture, gardens and plats attracted us even beyond warning notice-boards about 'daylight movement'. We were now to become acquainted with a mood of War which permitted no half-measures and no estaminets on the communication trench.

Marching well west of the battlefield, we saw unusual sights such as the aerodrome near Auchel, and I think a military mineral-water works before that. We were in high spirits, knowing nothing of the actualities we were making for. On the 13th we reached Monchy Breton, a dank village in the Arras area, out of which we marched for training on some breezy downs chequered with thick woods. Here was ground said to be just like that we were to attack in reality. Minute instructions were given, and followed by all ranks. Early on the 24th we were on the road again, and our march was assisted by a short train journey; the night we spent at le Souich ('Oh, *swish*'), and six hours dusty tramp next day brought us to Warnimont Wood at two in the afternoon. Reconnaissances at a front-line village called Hamel, on the River Ancre, detached some parties on the 26th and 27th, when all moved to P.18 or Mailly-Maillet Wood – a dishevelled little scrubbery viewed by German observation balloons and shelled unpleasantly. The battalion transport shared the wood and suffered from the shelling. After making its forward preparations, hindered by much rain, and after two postponements of the attack, the battalion filed into its assembly trenches on Hamel hillside by midnight of September 2nd. At 5.10 on the 3rd the attack began. The gunfire was heavier than we had known. I believe no one can say what happened to our bombing parties under young Lieut. French, who was to clear up the suspected German dugouts in the railway cutting. Nor is there much detail of our main waves. Led by Captain Northcote, a number of men went past the German front trenches, and formed an isolated post. The majority, under Captain Michell and 2nd Lieut. James Cassels, dug in nearer the German parapet. Nothing could be done to relieve the attack, which had collapsed north and south as well. The order to withdraw was sent in the afternoon but Northcote and his valiant companions were not successful in their attempt to recross no-man's-land. The battalion (relieved by the Cheshires) assembled in a trench along Hamel village street and in the setting sun arrived at Englebelmer, three hundred fewer in number than when it passed through that village the evening before. Temporary organization in two companies instead of four was found necessary. The survivors seemed scarcely to realize their survival; it was a dizzy end to an incredible day.

On the 6th we moved, no great distance, to Beaussart, where there were a few civilians whom the men distrusted. Reinforcements from England – four hundred men – were received here. Colonel Harrison rapidly restored the battalion to its normal working. On the morning of the 14th we took over the extensive trenches before Beaumont Hamel and once in appeared unlikely ever to get out. However, we were for the present secure from the painful chaos of fighting a few miles south. In these trenches (supported by the decaying positions of Auchonvillers) we worked hard and were shelled and trench-mortared not too violently most days; but the minenwerfers caused casualties. Gas-shelling on September 23rd may be noted; at that date, the only box-respirator in the battalion was at headquarters. To assist the troops in the attacks on Thiepval, southward, we put up rows of dummies in screens of smoke. On October 4th under a burst of shelling we were relieved, but only in order that we might make a circuit through Englebelmer Wood and Martinsart Wood on our way to the Hamel trenches. A party was sent up during this short interval to reconnoitre the region of Thiepval Wood, which was at that time intensely contested. Hamel was better. Moonlight nights threw a strange illusion over the Ancre valley, and autumn afternoons glowed among the wildflowers along our communication trench, Jacob's Ladder, which began at the poisonous spot Mesnil. The battalion occupied a front usually held by two battalions, and did this safely for ten days. A smoke barrage was produced by us and the trench mortars on October 12th to call off German attention from an attack south of the river. The Royal Naval Division relieved us on the 16th, but we immediately moved into Authuille Wood south of Thiepval and prepared for an attack. When the battalion occupied its assembly positions in the frosty muddy upland, on the 20th, it had been roughly five weeks without rest, and was greatly exhausted; nevertheless, at zero hour (12.7 p.m., October 21st) it advanced over the open with beautiful steadiness to seize Stuff Trench. It did what it was ordered to do, and held the trench until relief at midnight on the 22nd. The cost was two hundred and seventy-nine killed, wounded and missing. Among the killed was an especially cheerful and determined officer named Doogan. The state of the ground traversed by the battalion was extraordinary, and the mud-pools were strewn with corpses.

After the relief, some poor tents south of Aveluy Wood seemed remarkably comfortable; but on the 25th the battalion was holding the line again

(Thiepval Wood), and thereabouts it stayed, digging and carrying and being shelled, until the 30th. That morning it worked its way through heavy rain and a slough of despond past Thiepval village to Schwaben Redoubt. Here there was always some shelling, but on the 31st we were systematically bombarded, and when we were relieved (next day) the tour had cost us thirty-two casualties. The relief was expensive mostly to the Cheshires, whom the Germans saw coming in; the business, though simple in itself, took five hours. We rested in the cabin-like dugouts called Authuille Bluffs, on the steep rise from the Ancre inundations, and then did even better by getting back as far as Senlis. Two days, and we were at Thiepval Wood afresh, but quickly returned to Senlis and its barns and estaminets; on November 7th we were working in a winter storm in the Aveluy region, and on the 10th we resumed or were resumed by the Schwaben Redoubt, which was by now a few deep dugouts and a maze of crushed and choked trenches. We attempted a raid the night following, and by good luck caught two German soldiers without losing anybody. It was beyond the understanding of the men in the mud that an attack by us was imminent, but that was the fact, and on November 13th other units of our Division passed through our positions and overran, or overwaded, the German forts beyond. Our task should have been the melancholy one of carrying and dumping wire for the Division in front of its extreme advance, but there was such a blaze of shells bursting in no-man's-land in such a vile November night that we were let off and had to go no further with the materials than the old front line. This was the close of the battalion's Somme battle. One night at Pioneer road (huts along a sunk track), one at Warloy-Baillon (unspoiled houses with curtains and door-knockers), and then on the 15th a march of fifteen miles ending at Doullens. A train journey north, on November 17th-18th, removed us from the Somme area.

There one may define the end of the second part of this short history. During almost three months the battalion had been practically always under fire, had held trenches for scarcely tolerable periods and shared in three bewildering and devastating attacks. It had been cut off, with little exception, from common sights and scenes of life, and had become accustomed to two views of the universe: the glue-like formless mortifying wilderness of the crater zone above, and below, fusty, clay-smeared, candle-lit wooden galleries, where the dead lay decomposing under knocked-in entrances. The battalion had vastly changed in its personal composition under these prolonged tribulations; of the four hundred men who joined at Beaussart even, a great number were dead, wounded or otherwise vanished before we left the district.

In piercing cold the battalion occupied M Camp among Belgian farms and the huts of refugees, on the Poperinghe-Watou road, and refitted and drilled there until December 5th. When we left M Camp, it was not to try our fate at Ypres as we might have surmised but to find out still quieter places than Poperinghe. We went by train to St. Omer and by road to Moulle, near which place we built rifle-ranges. On December 15th, however, there was a train journey ending at the ruins of the Asylum, Ypres, and a turn in the trenches north of that city – Canal Bank. This period was one of the most peaceful and harmless that we ever had in the Line. On the 23rd we were sent back to E Camp in Elverdinghe Woods, and a snowy and joyful Christmas followed, in spite of the reconnaissances that day in the trenches of Boesinghe. There we relieved the 10th South Wales Borderers on the 30th, and the year 1916 ended for us in a dull commonplace trench day.

The Belgian Army were on our left flank at Boesinghe, where the front trench was cut in the raised Canal bank. So was the German trench over the frozen shallow Canal. Behind us was shapely clean country, and Elverdinghe Château was intact. We were encamped in its neighbourhood for almost a fortnight before a new and memorable experience – a first night in Ypres, to which we came after dark. Some were in the cellars of the Convent, others in basements near the old Station square. Next night we went through the Menin Gate to relieve trenches at Potijze; fierce cold prevailed and heavy snowfall. After four days 'in', we were relieved by our friends the 14th Hants, and sheltered in the same smoky recesses of Ypres, and went in and out for wiring and other work. Eastward again on the 24th – and we had hardly relieved the Hants and settled down to freeze in peace when a box barrage of minenwerfer shells and whizzbangs cut out our extreme right (a strong bombing post). The Germans had thought out a clever raid; their raiders apparently huddled in a culvert, under the railway by which our post was placed, until the moment of entry. Our men (it was evident later) fought hard, but we lost three missing, five killed, others wounded; three of the raiders were killed. The following evening a false gas alarm called down a bitter bombardment, and the next evening another false alarm produced a similar clash. There was great unrest, and we did our best to scour no-man's-land at night; and it was earnest winter weather. The guns and planes were restless as we. The 14th Hants succeeded us on the 28th, and we clanked down the road into Ypres, for more fatigues in the snow. The Germans raided the Hants next, and though we passed a further spell of Potijze (February 1st-4th) without such shocks, after we had gone out by train from Ypres to Vlamertinghe we still provided supporting companies in Potijze village, and reconnoitred emergency and alternative routes over open land to the front trenches. A German attack was apparently feared.

The Vlamertinghe camp was useful for battalion drill (where a hop garden had been), and vast quantities of fuel were burned there; on February 16th we entrained at the Cheesemarket, Poperinghe, on a little railway which took us to Bollezeele. Great cheerfulness ensued, and the winter relented at last; but such times sped by, and on the 24th we were at Winnipeg Camp, Ouderdom, on our way into the Salient again. Next day we moved to Ypres and Zillebeke Lake, a reservoir in the Bund of which were dozens of flimsy dugouts. Headquarters was a tall drab house at Kruisstraat, memorable to us as the last headquarters of Colonel Harrison while he was with us. Here he received an order to proceed to a Staff school in England. Almost at once the battalion suffered more troubles. The adjutant Captain Lintott – brilliant in the Somme battle – was compelled by illness to leave us. Then when the battalion, after a terrific struggle through the dark and storm, occupied trenches on Observatory Ridge, it was bombarded and raided, and lost sixteen killed and wounded. Among the casualties was the regimental sergeant major, Daniels; a shell burst in headquarters at Valley Cottages during the relief, and he died a few days later at Vlamertinghe. A great man.

Leaving Observatory Ridge, its bony stumps of trees and naked tracks, on March 3rd, the battalion was some days in Winnipeg Camp, and reconnoitred a reserve system at Dickebusch. It returned to Ypres by train but on nearing the town waited for a furious bombardment to slacken; once again it took over the Observatory Ridge trenches from the 14th Hants, amid bursts of rain and gunnery. Four days on the grill here, then four with night work at Kruisstraat, then Winnipeg Camp again, then the short train ride and the halt while Ypres was being further pulverized, and Observatory Ridge once more. This time the four days ended with the headquarters being driven out of Valley Cottages (a most dangerous solitary set of ruins) by the German gunners, and trying to find some better hole in the scarcely preferable raggedness of Zillebeke. This search the 14th Hants continued, during the night of March 31st; the battalion retreated into Zillebeke Bund. The snow reappeared, and betrayed the secret entrances to the dugouts of Observatory Ridge, where the battalion again took charge for four days. Emerging on April 7th, we found an alluring 'revue' being played by the 49th Divisional Follies in a vast hut at Brandhock, but as we drifted forth from it into the crystal light of evening we saw and heard a display of artillery in the St. Eloi direction which 'beat all'. Trouble was anticipated for us, and indeed for everyone in the region; but the German attack was limited and local. There were days in the Infantry Barracks at Ypres (stiff with big guns now); at Brandhoek again, among the farmers; and then in the wet the battalion manned trenches about Hill Top Farm north of Ypres. From these it moved back to the Canal Bank, then a sort of Garden City of pretty dugouts and many of them. The end of April approached, and another Allied Offensive was also thought to be approaching. We entrained at Ypres, passed through our old M Camp, entrained again on May-day and formed up outside St. Omer's distinguished-looking station. Marching on (with one night at Hallines), we found very humble billets in a cow-scented village named Zudausques, and were kept miserably and ironically busy with training in a new method of attack. In this manner May, 1917, went by; but halfway through we were transferred to Wormhoudt, where there is a hotel; but we saw little of it.

Inspected and trained to a degree, we next moved by road to D camp in the woods of Elverdinghe.

The Salient was becoming uglier all round. The battalion was helping to build railways for a few days, then held trenches – June 1st-6th – at Hill Top. At all hours spiteful bombardments were put down, and the first day brought fourteen casualties. There was gas on all sides, too, when the battalion came back to the Canal Bank; it was no sort of rest, and the next trench tour in a heat-wave had countless grim moments. No place was safe. Those trenches were not made for this power of artillery. On June 16th there was a midnight move to Elverdinghe, and on the 21st we went by train from Poperinghe station (listening to the explosions of shells in the station yard) to Watten and on foot from that dreamy village to even dreamier Houlle. This move was one of the wetter ones. At Houlle we were happy, beating down much promising corn with our practice offensive, swimming in the big ballast-holes, and approving the inexhaustible beer of the place. And this lasted three weeks and more before the offensive in question dragged us eastward. We arrived then by train at Poperinghe (passing new sidings, and hospitals!) and marched to C Camp, Elverdinghe. It was changed. Camps shelled, air duels, dumps exploding, new roads, tracks, light lines – these were the disorder of the day.

On July 22nd a patrol sent by us to Hill Top under an inexperienced officer disappeared, complete with maps and papers relating to the attack. Other patrols were sent up on later nights. The Canal Bank was full of gas. There were reports of a German withdrawal, but it was found not to be quite an innocent one. By night on July 28th the battalion marched into its assembly area – trenches old and new at Hill Top. Dreary continuous gunning accompanied us. On July 30th, waiting and preparing, at least seven of us were killed and six wounded. The skies had plenty of rain in them, despite liberal disbursements. On July 31st, at 3.50 a.m., as dark as could be, we attacked the demolished High Command Redoubt. The British barrage was such as numbed our powers of realization; the reply to it was instant, but diffused. The battalion took its objectives, and got busy with a line of shell-holes, shaping out some kind of posts; but the rain set in, and what the careful fire of the German heavies did not do the rain did. It rained all night, and through August 1st; and the German gunners, from their reserve positions, fired on with accurate diligence. By 3 a.m. on August 2nd the battalion had gone forward to relieve the 14th Hants in the Black Line, along the Steenbeek; a formidable day followed. Counter-attacks threatened, and were broken up. The German gunners did their utmost for their infantry, and all our headquarters were destroyed by direct hits. From this bad eternity we were relieved at night by the 17th K.R.R., and found our way to the far side of Canal Bank, a hot meal, and what sleep could be got. The blaze of dumps just behind was hardly noticed next day, and nobody was pleased with the prospect of further trouble in the front line; but we escaped that, and by train and road were sent to School Camp, St. Jans ter Biezen, beyond Poperinghe. An estimate of our total casualties in the action was two hundred and seventy-five.

The sun came out, and life improved; moreover, when the battalion decamped, it was to a fresh area, that of Meteren, the pretty spire of which looked along the highway to the Moorish steeple of Bailleul. Here a sort of divisional reunion happened, and the bands of several battalions played in the crowded streets; it was as though the spirit of the preceding year were challenging that of 1917. A move to Dickebusch on August 12th, and reconnaissances, preceded the return to the 1917 spirit of Spoil Bank (Hollebeke). Midnight at once produced shelling and gas, which affected everybody. On the 17th the battalion went forward into the shell-holes, not knowing where the Germans were (and the Germans were as well informed about it). Four days of that, and two at Spoil Bank again where the instantaneous fuse caused some losses; thence to Ridge Wood Camp, shells and showers. On the 27th the battalion relieved the Black Watch at Hollebeke (the operation took over seven hours); the dugouts surprised even us by their stench. A wind arose and dried the shell-holes, which was much appreciated. After this term of four days, relief only meant the homeless wreck of old trenches near Spoil Bank, but that was followed by some better days at Ridge Wood Camp.

In mid-September the battalion held the line at Mount Sorrel, and carried in materials for an attack; was in Divisional Reserve at Voormezeele; did four days' slogging in Larch Wood Tunnels. In that hideous neighbourhood, while some of the headquarters were waiting the word to proceed away from the line, a shell fell in their midst, killing seven of our best men. The names of the next camps which the battalion endured sound odd – Ascot Camp, and Beggars' Rest. From these withered, draggled places we moved into the true gehenna on the 23rd, and the next evening occupied the front line (no line!) south of the Menin Road. This quarter was called Tower Hamlets. The daytime was burning hot, the night subtly cold, and frantic shelling from 'the Tenbrielen Group' continued. On the night of the 24th a German attack drove in the battalion on our left, but Captain P.L. Clark saved our situation (a habit of his). On the 25th this position fighting continued, and on the 26th our brigade attacked and cleared some ruins of Gheluvelt outskirts. There had never been, in all our experience, such shelling; and the SOS signal went up north and south most monotonously. On the 27th at last one of the shells that hit the headquarters pillbox went through and killed six. How the Rifle Brigade relieved us in daylight, we scarcely knew. We halted a few hundred yards back in Bodmin Copse, and the copse was treated to measured and exact shelling from heavy howitzers. Gas shells came later, but we got away, and that night were carried on lorries from Bus House, St. Eloi, to Berthen, hilly and windy country. The casualties of this Menin Road tour were estimated at 200.

222

Now the usual restlessness of 'rest' ensued, parades, clearings, baths, exercises, and lastly reconnaissances. Mt. Kokereele was left behind reluctantly on October 15th, and on the way up to the battlefield a shell dropped among headquarters staff with deadly effect. In that district there was hardly time, or condition, for noticing who was dead. Round some deep water-logged tunnels called Hedge Street and Canada Street this was particularly the case. The battalion spent two nights in the Tunnels, then three in the front line, where once a stream called the Bassevillebeek had flowed. It now lurked in a yellow swamp. The front line was calmer than could have been dreamed, and the tour was lucky. The guns were fighting the guns rather than us. The German artillery ignored an SOS call from their infantry who took our being relieved to be an assembly for attack. We withdrew to Bois Camp, near Dickebusch Brasserie – a set of melancholy bivouacs; but we got a little warmer on October 21st (the anniversary of our Stuff Trench success) by marching to baths at Kemmel Château. It is not everyone who has a Château to bathe in. Two days after that distinction we were transferred to some old horse-lines near Reninghelst, which amounted to an involuntary cold bath; the wind howled and the rain flashed white. Odd jobs followed, and at least we were promoted to the decencies of Chippewa Camp on the 29th. From that place we went forward about October 31st to carry the customary 'materials' and dig a trench beyond Hill 60 – an operation well conducted (Col. Millward's headquarters were in Larch Wood Tunnels, one of the finest works of the kind). There was a lavishing of gas shells and general 'ironware' on our tracks; but on the morning of November 1st we were met by lorries in St. Eloi and so 'home'.

The name 'Tower Hamlets' had a pernicious sound for us, but to that point of the firing line the battalion was sent next (Nov. 3rd). Its chief performance was to throw smoke bombs, assisting operations at Polderhoek Chateau just north and Passchendaele farther off. A harmless relief followed, but when the battalion had gone as far back as Bodmin Copse a single shell killed three officers and N.C.O.s (I make no attempt to register all casualties; this is by way of example). On November 7th the battalion moved farther back to Godezonne, *vulgo* God's Own Farm, Vierstraat; and in the succeeding days it went, *via* Chippewa Camp and plenty of rain, to Bedford House, a mud-spot near Ypres. For the rest of the year 1917 the 11th Royal Sussex were mainly employed as workmen, under the direction of the Royal Engineers or our own Pioneers. A few days – November 25th to 29th – were granted at Winnizeele, almost civilization; on the 29th the battalion took a train at Godewaerswelde to Ypres. The train made good time, leaving at 8.55 a.m. and covering the dozen or more kilometres by 10 a.m. Encamped on the Potijze Road, the battalion built lengths of railway and causeway; all might have been friendly but for air raids. At 5.30 on the evening of December 6th, one bomb killed eight and wounded eight. These men thus missed the agreeable return from St. Jean station (a scarcely believable sign of the British advance) to Winnizeele and thence to the barns of Seninghem. There in spite of the eternal training programme and rifle-range, Christmas was, as they say, celebrated; on Boxing Day there were snowball fights.

The year 1917 ended with the battalion in Siege Camp, by Ypres. Siege Camp was left for Morocco Camp, another bleak place with a view of Passchendaele, of no touristic value. In rain and snow, from January 16th at dawn to dark on the 18th, the battalion held a few advanced mudholes at Westroosebeke. Trench feet (a crime) became a serious concern. For about a week the battalion remained in Hill Top Farm, among its memories of old trench tours and the initial Passchendaele attack, and in School Camp. A big move was in preparation, and, having entrained at Proven on January 26th, 1918, the battalion arrived after twelve hours at Mericourt, in the south of the British line.

Thus ended the battalion's principal connection with poor Ypres and her sad Salient. It had been a lengthy connection, and one which we should have wished to end sooner. It is true that through 1917, when we were not in the line, we were sent often enough to a considerable distance from it, and passed weeks in sleepy villages and safety. Moreover, philanthropy from above frequently caused one or other of us to be dispatched to one of the courses of instruction, far from enemies, that multiplied through this year. But the dreary dreadfulness of front line experiences now, the sense of a curse over and round Ypres, the 'looped and ragged nakedness' of forward camps, the air war on them, the apparent futility of the British effort, and the shattering of all unity by casualties beyond our counting, made that year at Ypres a bad business.

Invigorated by the prospect of a new front that, whatever it would be, was not Ypres, we moved forward past Peronne. By light railway, in a fantastic scene of trees bearded with hoar frost, and a ghostly silence, we came to the Cambrai battlefield and the ruins of Gouzeaucourt on a hill. We worked this subsector, between Revelon Farm as close support and the firing-line with its useful deep dugouts and keeps, until March 12th – about thirty-six days; and a great deal of digging, wiring and carrying was done besides the actual maintenance and defence of the positions. Originally calm, the place became noisy and deadly – there were tragedies on the duckboard tracks. On March 9th, crossing the wide no-man's-land, D Company entered the German trenches and found nobody. At last the battalion was taken out, and was busy for a few days finding its way about G.H.Q. Line, in Gurlu Wood and Hem; it was at Hem on March 21st. *Dies Irae*. Then came the Germans. The story hereabouts feels the strain. On the 21st-22nd the battalion was fighting and withdrawing at Villers Faucon, on the 22nd-23rd on a ridge near Bussu, then along the Somme Valley and across the river at Buscourt, and at Hem on the 24th. Reorganization at Chuignolles (March 25th), a withdrawal near Harbonnières (26th), through Harbonnières (28th), a Divisional concentration at Cayeux (noon of the 28th) – these are the dry bones of this episode. Then on March 29th the battalion faced the Germans at Wiencourt, withdrew to Ignaucourt, to a sunk road north of Aubercourt, to another south of Courcelles; on the 30th, it was driven back in the early morning and gradually retreated to the Villers-Bretonneux-Aubercourt Road. A fine position was taken up before the Bois de Hangard and improved at once; then on the last of March the 18th Division relieved. To collect what remained of the battalion was the next task, at Cléry and Amatre. The action had cost 20 officers, 300 other ranks killed, wounded and missing. On April 7th the unit marched twenty-five kilometres to Embleville and on the 9th entrained for Arques near St. Omer.

But rest was not yet. Ypres even was not done with. A day or two at Tatinghem, and there was a railway journey to Vlamertinghe. Toronto Camp, Otago Camp, and another march to Voormezeele, with its ugly associations. Here the battalion began a new trench system and had soon the chance to test it, the Germans (after several days of cannonading) attacking it early on April 25th. The shelling of Elzenwalle Château ruins was tremendous, and it was there that headquarters had placed themselves. On the 26th the battalion re-took from the Germans its old friend Dickebusch Brasserie. There were new alarms, assaults and barrages next day, but the King's Liverpools relieved that night, and the 11th went into support near Dickebusch Camp. The noise of battle, and more than noise, involved it even there, but it had a night or two at Devonshire Camp. On May-day, the battalion relieved in the front line. This tour ended on the night of May 3rd, and so far as I know that was the last time on which the 11th Royal Sussex as such had any concern with trench tours. By way of St. Jans ter Biezen and M Camp, well known resting-places, it was withdrawn to Nielles-les-Ardres, near Audruicq, which again is quite near Calais.

There the battalion was split up. Part of it was given the honour of instructing American infantry, and afterwards served in the mysterious campaign in North Russia. Arctic kit was finally handed in, and the whole history ended. Ended? Not while the Southdown battalions meet, as annually they do, to preserve their co-relationships. In sketching the movements of the 11th Royal Sussex overseas, I have hardly referred to the personalities who most of all would be mentioned among us when we gather now. I hardly know how to do it, without doing injustice to many others on whom, consciously or unconsciously, we relied. Let me remember Lieut. Swain, our unbeatable quartermaster, and one who was ever with us though not of us, our Brigade Commander, General Hornby. In my rapid chronicle there is nothing about the life and labours of our Transport, who never once let us down (we ate our iron rations at Stuff Trench, but there was some misunderstanding). Of the impressions we had, of every place and time we knew, I could not unprompted give a fair general account now; some we have mercifully forgotten in the main, others we have a trick of remembering. It is all so long ago now; and yet when I think of the 11th Royal Sussex on a winter evening, under all its ordeals or in any of its recreations,

Bare winter suddenly is changed to spring.

(1933)

Index of Titles and First Lines

Titles are given in italics

INDEX OF TITLES AND FIRST LINES